LET US BE
WHAT WE ARE

LET US BE WHAT WE ARE

The Joys and Challenges of Living the Little Way

Clarence J. Enzler

Christian Classics ✛ Notre Dame, Indiana

First published in 1978 as *Let Us Be What We Are*.

© 2012 by Ave Maria Press, Inc.

Founded in 1865, Ave Maria Press is a ministry of the United States Province of Holy Cross.

www.christian-classics.com

ISBN-10 0-87061-256-5   ISBN-13 978-0-87061-256-5

Cover image (necklace) © Hemera Technologies/Thinkstock.

Cover and text design by John R. Carson.

Printed and bound in the United States of America.

Library of Congress Cataloging-in-Publication Data

Enzler, Clarence J.
   Let us be what we are : the joys and challenges of living the little way / Clarence J. Enzler.
      p. cm.
   Includes bibliographical references (p.   ).
   ISBN-13: 978-0-87061-256-5 (pbk.)
   ISBN-10: 0-87061-256-5 (pbk.)
1. Spirituality. 2. Spirituality--Catholic Church. 3. Spiritual life--Christianity. 4. Spiritual life--Catholic Church. 5. Christian life. I. Title.

   BV4501.3.E595 2012
   248.4--dc23

                          2011045293

Contents

Preface to the Christian Classics Edition

Memorial Mass in honor of Rev. Dr. Clarence Enzler

Old Saint Mary's Church, December 6, 1976

Last spring, the father of one of our parishioners died in Massachusetts. On returning home to our parish, my friend told me how his brother, a priest, preached at the Mass of Christian Burial for his dad. His brother had said in the beginning of that homily that one of the deepest apprehensions a priest can have after ordination is the thought of presiding and preaching at the death of one of his parents. That task faces me today. I dare say few priests have had the opportunity to preach about a man as special as my dad.

In the past few days I have been given much solicited advice about this moment. Many have said that for me to preach is a task too big to tackle; I should ask one of Dad's dear friends instead. Others have told me to prepare the homily and never take my eyes from the written word in delivering the text.

There is no question that many others here this morning speak more eloquently and more to the point than I could. There is no doubt that my emotions might grab a hold of me as I express these words. But there are thoughts that must be shared this morning that could only be shared by a member of our family. My joyous task as a priest and member of the Enzler family is to speak once more for Dad in the name of the thirteen faith-filled people you see today in the first few pews of this Church. I'm sure you know that my words today will not be my words alone, but also those of the entire Enzler family.

My dad is known by so many in so many different ways that it is difficult to begin.

Some of you here today know him as a dedicated public servant to his country for thirty-two years as a writer for the Department of Agriculture. You know that he sweat blood in his desire to produce the best quality material for seven Secretaries of Agriculture.

Others know him as a member of Toastmasters where he learned to speak with such proficiency that he completely overcame a lifelong speech handicap and won international awards for his speeches. And as a speaker and homilist he was known throughout the Archdiocese for his ability to affect people and bring them closer to God by the spoken word. And even so, what he was spoke louder than his words.

Many others who celebrate with us this morning know him through his writings. *My Other Self, Everyman's Way of the Cross, In the Presence of God,* and his articles on the faith have set him apart as a writer par excellence. Those of you who have read his works know that he was a spirit-filled man of God who allowed Jesus to speak through him. In fact, it was while at the typewriter working on an article for the *Catholic*

Standard that he had the attack that took him to the hospital for the last time. How appropriate that one of his last acts of service to the Father was to use his gift of writing to bring the good news to the people of this Archdiocese.

Still others here today know him as a deacon. When the apostles chose the first seven deacons they called them to be men of service to the poor, the widowed, and the homeless. Dad found in his assignment at Old St. Mary's Church the opportunity to serve the poorest of the poor in both body and spirit. He was looked up to and loved by his fellow deacons who saw him as an example of service to them.

Many today reverence and remember Dad as the director of the Family Life Bureau. He touched so many through the many programs designed to help restore health to the family: Marriage Encounter, PreCana, Engaged Encounter, Post Cana, Teams of Our Lady, CFM, Cana Clubs, Natural Family Planning, Separated and Divorced Catholics, the Family Renewal Program, and Christinus. Though he obviously was not the main thrust behind all of these programs, even those not founded by him were deeply touched by the deft direction of his gentle hand. He often said, with his special kind of sincerity and vigor, that the most important apostolate in this Archdiocese is the family. If we take care of that apostolate, all else will fall into place.

There are very few here today who can't relate some experience of knowing Dad as a friend. A friend to many he was! He had that special talent of being concerned about any one and every one who crossed his path. The gift of himself was one anyone could share. It was given with no strings attached.

A few of you might know Dad in all of these capacities — public servant, toastmaster, homilist, writer, deacon, director of Family Life Bureau, and friend. But only one of us here today knew him as husband. And only thirteen of us knew him as dad. Even with all of his other accomplishments, his greatest gift of himself, his greatest contribution, was as husband and father. I guess it is hard for those of you who didn't share this special relationship of wife, son, or daughter to understand what he meant to us.

The greatest testimony any of us can give to Dad is that he taught us through his fatherhood on earth what it is to have a Father in heaven. Each of us learned about God's love for us through the love that Dad expressed to us from morning till night—and sometimes far into the night. Many other things could be said about our family life. I could talk about our dinners with fifteen gathered around a dining room table made for ten. It would be easy to talk about how we teased him and how he teased us. What love was shared in those moments. Who in our family can forget Christmas Eve when we would all be together, and Dad would say a line that has become very familiar in our home—"Isn't this fun!"

Only he could tell bedtime stories as he did—there were often stories from the Bible. Mom and Dad were inseparable. What lessons we learned from that. But over and above all that the fact remains, the greatest testimony any of us can give, the most profound lesson any of us learned, the deepest influence Dad had on us, is that in his love for us we learned of the Father's love for us. We know God is love because Dad was love to us. We believe because Dad believed. In the words of the blessing of the father at the Baptismal ceremony he and Mom were "the first teachers of their children in the ways of the faith . . . the best of teachers bearing witness to the faith by what they say and do in Jesus Christ our Lord."

Dad's special influence in our life was not just on the natural plane, but on the supernatural as well. The fact that he and Mom have given thirteen dedicated, firmly-committed followers of Christ to the Church is testimony enough. Dad was a man of faith.

In today's world, when one looks around and sees so many young people giving up the faith and turning away from this great gift of their parents, the Enzler children can't help but realize that the gift of our faith lives in us because of the example of Mom and Dad. The image of God in our lives is a beautiful image of love. That comes from God's gift of Dad to us, who taught us that his love is only an infinitesimal microcosm of God's love for us.

And so now the task comes to me to speak about death. I have much to say, but I could never express my faith as Dad has expressed his for us all in a homily given at my uncle Eddie Ford's funeral. So I would like to quote his words directly from that text. Here is what Dad had to say. We apply these words now to him.

> That man, whose mortal remains lie here in this casket, is a greater success than any of us here in this Church. He has finished the race. He has won the fight. He

has conquered. We are still running, still fighting, still striving.

He whom we call dead is also more alive than any of us here in this church. For death is not an end. It is not final. It is a beginning.

The awe-full truth—and I use the word "awe-full" in the sense of a truth which should fill us with reverence—is that once God gives life, our life will never end. Once God creates the spirit which inhabits our frail bodies, life goes on forever. We cannot stop it. We cannot annihilate it. It is there as a continuing fact that will never cease.

What, then, is death? It is when two worlds meet with a kiss: this world going out, the world of eternity coming in. It is something which does honor to a whole life. It is the signature which we and God together place on our mortal lives. It is the turning over of ourselves from time to eternity. It is not the cessation of life, but an accident in it. It is a changing of gears in the journey of life.

I like to think of this analogy. The life after death for those who love God is as superior to our present mortal life as our present life is superior to the life we had when we were in our mother's womb.

We had life in the womb—the same life we possess now. But not until after we were born did we begin to come into the fullness of earthy life. Similarly, the life we shall possess when we see God face to face is the same as the life of grace we now possess—but, oh, how much more wonderful it will be—how much more complete, how utterly perfect!

So though we mourn the loss of a loved one, we rejoice, we sing alleluias, we play trumpets, violins, and drums. We raise our voices to God. We wear white vestments. He is risen, Alleluia.

One final word from Dad to us, his family. It, too, comes from Dad's thoughts at Uncle Eddie's funeral.

> It seems to me that in the death of a husband and father there is something akin to the death of Jesus. On the night before He suffered Jesus said: 'There are many rooms in My Father's house, and I am going to prepare a place for you.'
>
> Is it too much to believe that when a husband and father precedes his family into eternity, he, like Jesus, goes steadfastly toward Jerusalem to prepare a place for those he loved so well here on earth?

Dad has gone ahead of us, not to Jerusalem but to God, and he will await us there.

May God's peace be with him, for he has brought peace to us.

Reverend John J. Enzler

Author's Note

Most of this book was written when I was convalescing at home after major surgery. Propped up in bed, I dictated into a tape recorder an hour or two each day. There followed, of course, some weeks of transcribing the tapes, reorganizing the material and editing it. Writing the book, therefore, presented few problems. I now know what it means to say that a book can practically write itself.

The only real problem is whether these reflections should be published or kept as a personal journal. Should something so intimate, so peculiarly between God and one's self be shared as a book is inevitably shared? How does the dictum of Francis de Sales apply that "the grace to conceal a grace is no small thing?" What am I to make of the advice of those to whom I have shown these pages who have persistently urged publication? Is this predominantly a work of self-glorification or is it one of painful self-revelation?

On the other hand, am I making too much of it? Is all this rather ordinary in terms of the spiritual life so that I exaggerate its significance simply because it happened to me?

I do not know.

I only hope, and pray, Lord, that if it should not be published, something occurs to make Your will clear. If You desire it to be made public, let it say what You wish, in honesty and humility.

Part One

Following
the Little Way

Chapter One

The Grace to Conceal
a Grace

My dear Lord, twice I have had the temerity to write in Your Name, using Your words as I imagined You would use them if You spoke to me as to Your other self. I have had the boldness to do this, although how bold it was I do not really know. Since You dwell in all who are one with You in Your mystical body, it does not seem too out of place that I should have taken this liberty.

Yet who am I to presume to speak ostensibly in Your Name?

If I have been bolder than I should have been, I am not afraid, however, because like Thérèse, I am confident that You forgive, permit, and even delight in boldness so long as it is inspired by love, by confidence, by trust in You.

What I seek to do now is quite different. I shall try to speak to You, Lord, in my own way from the depths of my soul. I

shall try to share my thoughts with You even though there is
no need to share what You already perceive more clearly than
I. No thought that I shall ever have was unknown to You a
thousand years before I came to be. What does the psalmist
say? "O Lord, you have probed me and you know me . . . you
understand my thoughts from afar . . . Your eyes have seen all
my actions; in your book they are all written; my days were
limited before one of them existed."

Yet just as those who truly love are not afraid and do
not consider it time wasted to say to one another what each
already understands full well, so I shall do. But I know, Lord,
that I share these thoughts with You not for Your benefit but
for mine.

You know, dear Lord, it was decided a few weeks ago that
I should undergo surgery, because the problems I was having
with a grossly enlarged prostate gland were so severe that I was
being ground into exhaustion. Being able to sleep for only four
or five hours night after night, and being under the pressures
that the prostate condition also produced during the day, was
rapidly debilitating my energies, as well as making me irritable
and hard to live with. So it was determined that surgery was in
order. And since the gland was enormously large the operation
would require an abdominal incision, necessitating a stay of
some two weeks in the hospital and a period of rather complete rest for an additional three to six weeks after I returned
home.

You know, also, Lord, that a fortnight or so before I was
to enter the hospital I became filled with dread of the ordeal,
not just fear but dread, extreme apprehension. It was not that

I feared the possibility of death. Truly it seems to me that I love You enough and trust You so completely that death in itself has no terror for me. I believe I am totally honest in saying, Lord, that my only regret at leaving this mortal life would be the grief that would inevitably come to my dear ones: to Kathleen, our thirteen children who are Your gifts to us, their husbands and wives who are now also our sons and daughters, and my sister and brothers; also, of course, the dear friends who have become part of me as I am part of them; and in a particular way those who are my fellow members of Your clergy, Your priests and my fellow deacons.

Except that they would feel loss, I say the prospect of coming totally into Your arms and being permitted to see You with an intellectual gaze, as Paul says "face to face," holds only joy.

Why, then, did this impending surgery occasion so much alarm? Well, You will remember, dear Lord, some years ago when I underwent an operation to replace the detached retina of my left eye. At that time, almost twenty years ago, the patient, both before and after surgery, was required to lie on his back for days on end. When the time came to begin to bring the patient back to his feet he was raised up in bed and gradually reaccustomed to sitting and then to standing upright. Usually some nausea was involved and sometimes vomiting, but it quickly passed.

When, after some three weeks on my back I began to be raised to a sitting position, I immediately became most violently nauseous. Day after day the doctors and nurses tried to bring me to a sitting position, without the slightest success. No matter how gradually they raised me, nothing availed.

Sometimes, even after they gave up the effort for the moment and replaced me flat in bed, I retched and regurgitated so explosively that some particles struck the ceiling and others shot out fifteen feet across the room. They tried all the remedies they could conceive of, beginning with such simple ones as motion sickness pills and culminating in the suggestion that I go through the cancer clinic. I became dehydrated and they gave me glucose intravenously. For eight days this condition continued. It was the most excruciating, agonizingly painful, and enervating experience of my entire life. Fortunately, the retina held.

As I thought of this new surgery, wondering if a similar situation would develop, I became anxious, then worried, and finally almost obsessed with foreboding until it was with true dread, not just fear, that I approached the ordeal.

Then, Lord, as You do so often in Your care of us, a care that we accept unthinkingly, You provided the answer. For a long time I have been devoted to little St. Thérèse. It was reading her *Story of a Soul* that helped bring me closer to You many years ago by seeming to strike fire in my own soul. I know that the book in the edition available at that time was saccharine, naive, emotional, and, from a literary perspective, in some respects poorly written. But it has moved more persons toward goodness, inspired more to selflessness, urged more to seek You in love than perhaps any work published during this century. It is in the last two sections, especially as now officially translated by Ronald Knox, that the book becomes truly the story of a soul.

Both these portions were written within approximately the last year of her life. The first, done in a period of three days in September 1896, elaborates on her "little way"—coming to You by offering You all the small gifts of life. The other, written mostly between the beginning of June and early July of 1897, reveals some of the innermost secrets of her relationship with You, Lord, and speaks very intimately of Your loving care.

Under the inspiration of Your Holy Spirit, at the height of my dread, I came again on the story of St. Thérèse of Lisieux. I was looking at some of the books on the shelves of my library and You seemed to say to me, "Read this again, and it will help you."

I picked up the book and began to leaf through it. I was not interested in rereading the first portion, but beginning with the second part I began to read one chapter every day. You know what happened, Lord. I lost all fear of the operation. Totally, completely, effectively You removed every vestige of dread, fear, even anxiety.

I don't know exactly when all of this occurred. I do know that within two days at most, not only had anxiety departed, but I began to look to my surgery with a sense of anticipation as something that I was being privileged to offer to You. In addition, I felt urged to try as conscientiously as I could to imitate all the aspects of Thérèse's little way for which You gave me opportunity.

You know, dear Lord, how beautifully she speaks of the vocation of love. How does she express it? "Love is the vocation which includes all others." I cannot say that I had, as Thérèse did, a restless ambition to be for You everything at once: apostle, missionary, priest, victim, soldier. But what did strike me strongly again—as it had so often in the past—was her confidence in You and the inspiration to do what she had done. To ask that all Your saints obtain for me not only a portion of their love of You, but a double portion, so that like Thérèse, I could love You with all, and even more, of their loves combined; and even to go on to ask You to obtain for me all of Your own love so I could return it to You. I don't mean that there was anything remarkable in this, surely nothing mystical. But my whole attitude toward the surgery and also toward my daily life suddenly and dramatically changed.

Lord, I have often wondered about the understandings and lights that You give me. I used to accept as a matter of course, that everyone, at least everyone who showed any regard for You, received lights of this nature. I thought that I just had the temerity, the boldness, even the bad taste to reveal them, whereas others kept them in their inmost hearts where perhaps they belonged. Now, I don't know what I believe in this respect.

Ever since I read years ago the remark of Francis de Sales, another of my spiritual heroes, that "the grace to conceal a grace is no small thing," I have wondered about the wisdom of writing as I have done and am now doing. You know, Lord, that there can be terrible danger in writing about the inmost thoughts that You give us. People think of one as a holy person for expressing these insights. Even though one has a sense of unworthiness, there is the insidious temptation finally to accept the smug notion that one really is "holier than others." I remember, dear Lord, that when *My Other Self* was published I wished to have it appear anonymously or under a pseudonym so that no one would know I was the author. I still wish at times that I could have remained anonymous.

I recall how mortified I was one day when I happened to be in a rather large gathering—it was the occasion of our daughter Carol's graduation from college and I was the commencement speaker. The crowd was milling around outside the auditorium after the commencement ceremony when a young nun came rushing up to me, all in good will I'm sure, and said something to the effect that "no one could have written about prayer as you did in *My Other Self* without surely being in the unitive way." Persons in that day still spoke of the purgative, illuminative, and unitive ways.

What I replied I don't recall, but I probably stammered foolishly—I hope I did, so that she would see what a fool I really am.

One reason, perhaps the major one, that I put my name to *My Other Self* was a growing conviction that it would be cowardly not to do so. Somehow, Lord, I knew that *My Other Self* would achieve a wide circulation and the thought that there would be some notoriety attached to this was not at all attractive to me. Here I was, an employee in one of the large agencies of the federal government, and I envisioned myself being pointed out as a kind of holy Joe, a religious nut, someone so

queer as to profess openly to the world that he was in love with
You. I shrank from that. I was afraid that people would think I
was better than I am; yet I have to confess that another part of
me was proud enough to want people to think of me as better
than I know I am. Pride is always breaking out in me.

For better or for worse, the book did come out under my
name, though without any further identification. I'm sure
some persons who know me only from the book have vastly
exaggerated notions about me. But fortunately, once they
meet me, they quickly come back to reality.

To show the really horrible menace of spiritual pride, however, You know, Lord, what happened when I was working on
Everyone's Way of the Cross. I began this as a true labor of love
for You. I wanted to make it the finest piece of writing of my
life. If the total time given to the preparation and writing of
the fourteen stations could be added up, I believe it would
average out to many hours per word.

Again I felt sure that *Everyone's Way of the Cross* would
become extraordinarily popular. Well, You know how it is with
me, Lord, in my spiritual writings. Things go along famously
for a while, then everything seems to come to a dead stop;
sometimes for months on end, not another word is written.
This is what happened with *Everyone's Way of the Cross,* as it
had also with *My Other Self.* As I lay in the doldrums of my
spiritual writing, an anxiety, then a worry, and finally a fear
grew in me that someone else would come out with a modern

Way of the Cross before mine. Truly I became quite excited, quite upset, at this possibility.

Imagine, Lord, here was a work that I had begun for You and now it had become so much *my* work that I was no longer nearly as concerned about producing something that would lead others to love You as I was about being first with a work that would bring credit to me.

I'm sure it was only because of Your great love and mercy and because, being human, too, and having been tempted also by the sight of the world at Your feet that You did not withdraw from me further insights that would have made that little pamphlet impossible.

I cringe with shame when I think of how I betrayed Your trust in thus misusing Your gift. I know You have long since forgiven me, Lord, but again I beg Your pardon.

Yet even that lesson was not enough. When *In the Presence of God* was published, far from debating whether or not my name should appear as its author, I wrote in my own hand the boastful blurb on the flyleaf. Worse, I took pride in it. How far I had fallen from that earlier state in which You were my only interest in writing!

Again, Lord, I ask You to forgive me for making myself better than I am, for claiming for myself gifts that belong only to You.

As I compare *My Other Self* with *In the Presence of God,* I have no doubt that the latter is far more profound. You know, Lord, the years I spent in writing the short section on the Trinity, the thousands of pages I read and pondered, the hours of meditation involved. And You know also the somewhat shorter time, but years nevertheless, that went into the sections on the Incarnation and the Eucharist. Yet, *In the Presence of God* has proved attractive to only a small fraction of the number who have read and who continue to read *My Other Self.* Could it be, Lord, that this is Your way of telling me that what I did for You in the first book, because it was done for You, is more important in Your sight, and therefore You have made it more important in Your work than the second book that was done for You, yes, but also all too much for me?

Well, what of this present work that I am now putting on tape? For whom am I doing this? Dear Lord, I hope You know that it is for You alone. I believe I can say with total truth at this moment that I care not the slightest whether anyone shall ever see what I am now doing. Please, Lord, let it stay that way. Do not let me fall prey again to pride, and if it should happen that I do give way and begin to work more for myself than for You, quickly call me back. If it is Your will, I am perfectly resigned that whatever I do should be destroyed or, if not, that it be used by You to show others the trap that pride is always setting for the unwary.

How easy it is to fall. We are indeed weakest when we think we are strongest, and strongest when we realize that we are the weakest of the weak. Only when we begin to understand like Thérèsè the glory of being Your weak one, Your insignificant one, Your fledging bird as she expressed it, only then do we begin to be like the little children You have warned us we must become.

Chapter Two

Thérèsè's Little Way

Well, I have gone far afield. Let me get back to how You and Your Holy Spirit, in the Father's love, helped me to begin again the practice of the little way.

As Thérèsè points out, love needs to be proved by action. She uses the example of a little child scattering flowers that fill the room with their fragrance; and again of a little child singing in its shrill treble the great canticle of love. You know how she goes on to say that this would be her life, to scatter flowers, missing no single opportunity of making some small sacrifice, here by a smiling look, there by a kindly word, always doing the tiniest things and doing them right for love.

"I shall suffer all that I have to suffer—yes, and enjoy all my enjoyments, too—in the spirit of love so that I shall always be scattering flowers before your throne; nothing that comes my way but shall yield up its petals in your honor."

To those of us who are not childlike, this may seem naive. Yet her words, even as they had done many times before, plucked at the strings of my spirit. I am perfectly willing to admit, as she did, that it seems a bit like a childish game to be playing. Yet I think wisdom tells us in the idiom of the day that it is really the only game in town, the only game worth playing, the only thing worthwhile.

So, I, too, began to scatter little flowers, make little sacrifices, things that years ago I used to do a hundred and more times a day but that more recently I had been neglecting. Oh, I don't mean that I have not continued to make sacrifice. Anyone who loves You does that. But I did not offer little gifts of love in the profusion that now, once again, became my daily life. It seems to me that You began to call my attention continually to hundreds of small ways in which I could show my love for You; things so insignificant as picking a paper clip or a scrap of paper off the floor not because it needed doing but simply to show my love; or leaving my air conditioner off on a hot day; or being thirsty and foregoing a glass of water for an hour or so.

Of course, there were many other ways of scattering these little flowers. You know, Lord, how a good friend and I delight in bantering with each other. We've had a little game of seeing who could surpass the other in repartee or some clever bon mot. Now it suddenly became a great delight for me purposely to let him have the better of me and to watch his smile as he realized that he had won our little battle of words. I do not mean to imply in anyway, Lord, that his satisfaction was smug or complacent. He's not that kind of person as You know far better than I. He is truly a humble person. But he did take a kind of pure joy in coming out ahead in these small encounters.

Of course, as it happened, I gained far more joy in losing than I could ever have had in winning. You also gave me the grace not to let me become obvious; at times I would do my best in these engagements and would only withdraw from the field at the very last moment; and sometimes not even then.

Then there were the numerous occasions when I was about to offer a word of criticism or reproach, or perhaps only a reproving look in my dealings with co-workers, neighbors, friends, or family. You gave me the strength to smile brightly and either say nothing or pass off the occasion with the lightest of remarks. How gracious and amiable You help us to be, Lord, when we try to scatter little flowers in Your name.

Even more frequent than refraining from criticizing were the occasions to pay sincere little compliments, or to register pleasure by a smile, a wink, a raised eyebrow, a little gesture of head or hand.

There was one incident, dear Lord, that was quite similar to something that Thérèse related as one of her successes in practicing her little way. She said that at evening prayers her place was just in front of a sister who had an odd way, the moment she came into chapel, of making a curious little noise "rather like what one would make by rubbing two shells together." She says nobody noticed it except her, but that she simply could not describe how much that tiny noise bothered her. How she longed to turn around and give the offender a reproving look.

"But something told me," she says, "something deep down inside me—that the right thing to do was to put up with it for the love of God and spare the sister any embarrassment. So I stayed still and tried to get closer to God. Perhaps I could forget it altogether, this tiny noise."

But it was useless. "There was I," she goes on, "with the sweat pouring down me in the attempt to make my prayer into the prayer of mere suffering! Suffering—but somehow I must get rid of the nervous irritation and suffer peaceably, joyously, that is, with peace and joy deep down in my soul. So I hit on the idea of trying to *like* this exasperating noise, instead of trying vainly not to hear it. I devoted myself to listening hard, as if the sound were that of some delightful music, and all my prayer—it certainly wasn't the prayer of quiet!— consisted of offering this music to our Lord."

Something akin to this, I say, occurred to me. As You well know, Lord, I have the habit of going to noon Mass on Saturdays at one of our neighborhood churches. For months there has been a somewhat elderly woman at these Masses who prays out loud in a kind of monotonous mumble. She continues to do this throughout the Mass. Even during the canon, when everything is stilled except the voice of the priest, she goes on mumbling her prayers. It is like the hum of a bee or wasp in the room or like the exasperating buzz of a large fly in one's bedroom at night after you have turned out the light and are trying to get to sleep.

Sometimes she mumbles during the homily, and later, as the congregation comes down the aisle to receive You Lord, in Your glorified Body and Blood, there she is continuing to drone on even as she nears the priest to communicate.

It disturbed me so much that, like Thérèse, I wanted to turn and glare at her. Most times I resisted, but I am not as strong willed as Thérèse and two or three times I did look rather questioningly in her direction. In any event, looking or not looking had not the slightest effect on my unwitting tormenter. It may have been, again like Thérèse, that I was more sensitive to the disturbance than others.

I took to sitting in various parts of the church, hoping that by removing myself sufficiently I would escape the distraction. But my ears must have been peculiarly attuned to her wavelength because no matter where I sat, no matter how far away, I could still hear the droning and it seemed equally loud. Either this church has the most remarkable acoustics of any edifice I have ever been in or—or what; I don't know.

I must say, Lord, that I had tried earlier some of the techniques described by Thérèse. I, too, sought to sublimate the sound, even to make a kind of music out of what was almost the antithesis of music. All to no avail.

Then, under the influence of this new spiritual climate into which You had brought me, I decided that on this day when I went to the noon Mass I would sit either directly in front of or immediately behind her. I chose to sit behind rather than before because I was afraid that if I were sitting in front, I might be unable to resist the impulse to turn on her.

Lord, You know what happened. Throughout the Mass she made not one sound. I thought perhaps someone had spoken to her, told her how disturbing her habit is. Maybe. It seems likely. But no matter! There was no droning; no, as I used to think sometimes when the noise had gone on incessantly, "moaning at the bar." I'm curious to know what will happen when I am able to return to the noon Mass as soon as my recovery permits. (The mumbled praying continues, only it doesn't seem as loud now and it really doesn't bother me; most times I hardly notice it.)

It seems most appropriate for me to apply to this incident the words of Thérèse herself, "You can see for yourself that I am a very insignificant person, who can't offer You anything but very insignificant sacrifices."

But again I am getting far afield. I want to thank You, Lord, for making those days preceding my operation when I was practicing the little way with all my heart one of the happiest periods of my whole life. And of course, I thank You, dear Lord, for removing so totally any dread of my approaching trial. Truly I felt, "What have I to fear? You are with me. Though a thousand encamp against me, I will fear no evil." Not only had I nothing to fear, I truly had joy in looking forward to the moments that were to come, when I could offer You with all the love of my heart whatever pains my surgery might bring.

Several days before the operation was to take place a remarkable change occurred in my condition. Whereas before my symptoms had been extraordinarily severe, so that I would be up half the night trying to relieve myself with very inadequate success, now suddenly for a period of about a day-and-a-half there came an immense outpouring of fluid so that I couldn't believe where it was all coming from. Thereafter I began to have no difficulty sleeping through the entire night without ever getting up. In addition, whereas before on rising in the morning there had been a period of an hour or more before I became reasonably comfortable, now the problem was minimal, almost nonexistent.

I mentioned this change to Kathleen who, of course, had already observed it. After it continued for a couple of days I called my doctor and good friend, Jack Bresette, to explain the situation. He said, probably testing me, "Maybe we shouldn't go through with the operation at this time."

I asked if there was any possibility of the change being permanent.

"I don't think so," he replied. "For some reason the bladder, which our x-rays show has been emptying only about halfway, has suddenly been drained. But in all probability the situation will build up again, whether in a week, a month, or six months."

"Well, Jack," I said, "if you think the surgery will almost surely have to be done within six months, a year, or even two years, I'd sooner get it over with now."

"I think that's the wise decision. It's what I would advise," he said. "So let's proceed as planned. Meantime, watch the situation and call me again in a few days. When you come into the hospital we'll have another thorough examination and decide at that time what's to be done."

My improved condition continued almost unabated, except that I did begin to have a little more discomfort. Kathleen asked me, "Have you been praying for a miracle?" I said, "Not once." Actually, it had been about the farthest thing from my thoughts.

Dear Lord, You know I'm telling the truth when I say that while I had no idea what was going on within me, I was not really pleased with the improvement I had been experiencing. The thought of not being able to offer You this sacrifice of love was disappointing. I *wanted* to do it. I wanted to demonstrate my total willingness to suffer for You. I wanted to join my small pains to Yours in Your mortal life, to help fill up, as Paul said, what was lacking in Your suffering, to offer my sacrifice for the good of the whole Church, to join my few pangs to those of all Your saints and martyrs who have shown how easy it is with Your help to overcome human weakness. (Speaking of making up for what was lacking in Your sufferings, Lord, I now see this in a new way. You never grew old enough to have a prostate problem.)

And yet I knew that if it should be Your will that somehow some change had occurred that would make surgery unnecessary I would accept that, too, with gratitude and joy. But, Lord, do You remember my thinking while all this was going on: What if there *has* been some miracle? And my reaction: "Oh, no. Not that! By no means do I want to be singled out and pointed to as one who has been blessed by You in such an extraordinary way. Not that, Lord. Not that."

I thought of Teresa of Avila and how mortified she was at the extraordinary things You sometimes did to her publicly.

I don't believe that I put it into words, Lord, but I think the prayer of my heart was, "Please, dear Jesus, don't let this happen to me."

Perhaps somewhere deep in my spirit I had the feeling that motivated Philip Neri to keep saying, "Lord, beware of Philip." Lord, beware of me lest I betray you.

Chapter Three

Holy Week

About a week before surgery, You permitted Your Holy Spirit to cause me to think about how I could unite my ordeal with Your Passion and death. It occurred to me that surgery was scheduled for Friday at 11:30 and I thought it would probably get underway around noon, or the hour when traditionally we think of You as being nailed to the cross where You would hang for three hours. I began to think about what You had done during the first days of Your Holy Week and I wondered if there were ways in which I could, in a very insignificant manner, of course, relive with You that period and make these few days a holy week of my own.

Through Your immense kindness, Lord, I became increasingly conscious of the striking truth expressed by Thomas Aquinas, that Your actions in Your mortal life, and most notably in Your Passion and Death, have the same effect for one who unites his will with Yours as the actions of a man in the state of grace have for the man himself.

I'm saying it very poorly, but the idea is that because of the mystical oneness that exists between You and Yours, what You did is as though they had done it themselves. I was thinking that the corollary is that what we do in Your name is as though You had done it; and now I had something of my own, something significant, to hold up to You. Even though I know it is love that makes an offering significant, not its "size" in human terms, still the idea of a holy week to be joined to Yours greatly appealed to me.

The first day of my holy week was not Passion Sunday, or what we used to call Palm Sunday, commemorating Your triumphal entrance into Jerusalem. No, my holy week began with Trinity Sunday.

Somehow it seemed even more appropriate that this should be true. Although Trinity Sunday—in the estimation of most Christians—is not as great a feast, at least in terms of celebration and enthusiasm, as Easter, Christmas, and Pentecost, yet, am I wrong, Lord, in believing that Trinity Sunday is really the most basic feast of all, just as the doctrine of the Trinity is the most fundamental of all Christian beliefs? It is indeed from the Trinity that all else flows.

So I was pleased that my holy week should begin with this great feast. I had the privilege of preaching at Old St. Mary's Church that day, and, of course, I spoke on the Trinity. I remarked, and please, Lord, forgive me for going on like this, that the modern world is fascinated by mystery, riddles, and puzzles, as is evidenced by the tremendous sales of mystery novels and the enormous amount of time people spend in working crossword puzzles, solving anagrams and riddles of every variety.

I pointed out that the greatest mystery of all, the deepest puzzle and enigma, is the Trinity—the enormous mystery of one God and three co-equal Persons. I asked the people if they realized at all why You, Lord Jesus, revealed this mystery to us.

In speaking on the Trinity, of course, I had to meditate on it, going back to that section in *In the Presence of God.* Do You mind, Lord, if I recall now some of those thoughts?

Why is the Trinity so vital to Christian belief? Is it not because it is through the Trinity that we come to know You?

We can learn something about You, our God, from the universe, the innumerable galaxies and the billions of stars within each galaxy, the incredible age of the universe, including the five or six billion years that science tells us marks the lifespan up to now of our own, inconceivably vast and yet, in terms of the whole universe, inconceivably small solar system.

We can learn about Your power and Your wisdom, O God, not only from the stars but from the atom; and from life, our own human life and the lives of the birds, the beasts, the fish, and all those creatures of which the psalmist speaks with such beauty. But there is no way except through revelation that the human mind could conceive of Your wonder as expressed in the Trinity.

But why did You want us to know You? Was it not because just as a lover wishes to share his inner self with the person loved, so You longed to share with us the knowledge of Your own inner life? Because You love us You told us about the Trinity.

You did it to reveal Yourself, not only as man but as God. Human eyes could see You as man. If we were to know You, however, as You are, as God, You had to tell us about God. How could You be the Son Person of God unless there is also a Father Person?

You said plainly that Your Father and You are one. How could this be unless there are distinct divine Persons who are yet united as one Being?

How could You promise to send a consoler, a guide, a benefactor, who, as God Himself, would enlighten us about all things, without revealing the existence of Your Holy Spirit and His oneness with the Father and the Son?

But the answer to why You revealed the Trinity goes even further, does it not, Lord? In Your immeasurable love, You revealed the Trinity so that we Your creatures could know who we are, sons of God, and so we could begin to understand our sonship. The fact that You, Son of God and son of man, have one and the same Father in heaven is the key to our understanding that we also have a true Father in heaven. Only when we begin to see ourselves in relation to the Trinity can we come faintly to understand the glory that we already possess here on earth.

Finally, is it not true, Lord, You revealed this most intimate secret of the Godhead as a pledge that someday You would introduce us, "face to face," to the Father and the Holy Spirit and Your own Divine Person? Even here in this mortal life, You want us to know the great God not merely as He shows Himself in creation, but as He is in His inner life; and from that knowledge to begin to glimpse, very darkly to be sure, the immeasurable joy that is in store for us when we shall see You as You are.

The triumphal story of salvation seemed to me to be the most fitting entrance possible to my very little holy week that I felt You were giving me the privilege of joining to Yours. Did I thank You for making that Trinity Sunday so meaningful? If I did not, Lord, please accept the gratitude I feel and express now.

To unite my week more closely to Yours, dear Lord, I reread some of the accounts of the last days of Your mortal life. I had already done this a couple of months earlier during the actual Holy Week, because, as You know, it has been my custom for some years to relive mentally the events as narrated by Prat, Ricciotti, and others of the days immediately preceding Your Resurrection. So I did not have to read as intensively this time to recapture those events.

Everyone agrees that Monday and Tuesday of Your Holy Week were days of intense activity for You. You seemed to be calling one last time to those who had rejected You, making an almost desperate plea to them not to continue to reject Your message of love and salvation. And so You had Your encounters with the Herodeans, the Sadducees, and the Pharisees.

It was a head-on collision, because they were seeking You out also, trying to find a way to involve You with the Romans and thus do away with You or, failing that, to turn the people against You. So the Herodeans sought to entrap You by asking whether or not it was lawful to pay taxes to Caesar. You disposed of this question to their discomfiture and perhaps to their grudging admiration.

The Sadducees then came forward with their proposition about seven brothers, all of whom married the same woman after each of the brothers died in turn; and their question was: to whom would the woman belong in the day of resurrection? Again You turned the proposition against them with the comment that they understood neither the Scriptures nor the power of God.

Finally, the Pharisees, hoping to involve You in a controversy over the heavy and the light precepts of the Law, sent a scribe versed in the knowledge of the scriptures who asked, "Master, which is the great commandment?" You simply referred to the profession of faith written on the phylacteries worn by the Pharisees that says: "You shall love the Lord your God with your whole heart and with your whole soul, with your whole mind and with your whole strength." This, You said, is the first and the greatest commandment. And the second is like to it: "You shall love your neighbor as yourself." On these two commandments, You said, depend the whole Law and the prophets.

Then You posed a question. "How is it, that the messiah who is the son of David is called by David 'Lord'," as is written in the Book of Psalms. "'The Lord said to my lord, sit down at my right hand till I place all your enemies as a stool beneath your feet.' If David himself, therefore, calls him his Lord, how is he his son?"

They had no reply. So You began to hammer at their minds with the parables of rejection—the two sons, one saying he will obey his father but not doing so; the other saying he will not obey but then doing the task given him; the king who invited guests to the wedding feast of his son but they all had excuses and would not come; and the parable of the owner of a vineyard who rented it out to vine dressers while he went on a journey.

If they failed to grasp Your meaning in the first two parables, they could not escape it in the third. As Yahweh sent his prophets, so the vineyard owner sent his servants to claim the fruits that were his; but the vine dressers seized them, beat one, stoned another, and slew a third. As Yahweh sent other prophets so the owner sent other servants who met the same fate. Finally the owner sent his own son; and they "laid hold of him and they killed him." When You asked the Pharisees what the owner of the vineyard would do to those wicked men, they replied that he would destroy them. And You asked, "Have you never read in the Scriptures, 'the stone which the builders rejected, that same stone has become the corner stone.'" And You said that the kingdom of heaven would be taken from them and given to a nation that would yield its fruits.

Then, indeed, in their rage they would have seized You but for the people. Was it at that juncture, Lord, because of their hypocrisy, that You rebuked them in the series of terrible woes? Was this Your one final monumental effort to awaken these proud unbelievers to their wickedness?

How clearly You made me see, Lord, reading again the story of Your activities that Monday and Tuesday of Your Holy

Week, that even on the brink of death, You did not stop, but redoubled Your efforts to finish the teaching Your Father had commissioned You to do.

In my own insignificant way, I tried to imitate You. My doctor had said that I should get as much rest as possible in the days preceding surgery. But Monday is novena day at Old Saint Mary's Church. So in imitation of You, as I hope and believe, I went like You into the "temple," assisted as deacon at Mass, and stepped into the pulpit to lead the novena and preach my homily; and finally I gave Benediction of the Most Blessed Sacrament.

I could not help thinking that perhaps this would be the last time I would do those things. So it was with particular devotion that I raised high the monstrance containing Your glorified Body and blessed the people in Your name, looking at You the whole time, begging You to heed the prayers of Your people and thanking You from my heart for the immense privilege I had of being Your minister of the Most Blessed Sacrament.

I remember offering to You again, as I had so many times in the past few days, this little sacrifice of my surgery. Standing in the pulpit and looking at the life-size crucifix at one side of the church, I said to You: "My Friday is coming, too. I join whatever insignificant, miniscule, unworthy of notice pains and discomforts I may have to those which You endured for me and for all humanity." And I remember thinking: when the ordeal comes, if I should prove to be a baby, Lord, making much more of my little sufferings than many another person would, please accept here and now my willingness to offer everything totally to You with joy, not with mere resignation but with love of Your will. I tried to make the firm resolution that whatever You might send to me I would not change by one iota. I went home that night with a heart at peace and serenely joyful.

On Tuesday I did indeed stay home and rest. But I tried to pray more than usual, and I tried also to redouble the sacrifices of my little way. Humanly I wish I could remember more about that Tuesday, but it seems to have become obscured from my memory. Since that is the case, it is probably the way You want it; certainly it is what You permitted to happen. So I am content to let the Tuesday of my little holy week be lost in You and almost blank in my own memory.

Chapter Four

Surrounded by Love

It was on Wednesday, shortly after noon, that I entered the hospital. Something happened that morning that resembled one of the incidents of the Wednesday of Your Holy Week. It was on that day that the leaders of the priests and elders of the people met at the house of Caiphas to discuss what they should do about You. Apparently, on that day also, Judas came to them offering to deliver You into their hands.

That morning, while Kathleen went to the office, I stayed home. About mid-morning I received a letter publicizing an event that I had been planning myself, and that had evidently been taken over, without my knowledge, by a person whom I had liked and whose career I had helped. This person was aware of my policies and plans, and I would have assumed his loyalty. I could hardly believe that this was happening. But there was no mistake. I had not been informed or consulted, and it was evident that this project had been conceived, planned, and engineered totally behind my back, even though it dealt with a subject of primary concern to me. There could be no question but that I had deliberately been kept in the dark. It was a stab in the back by a friend. I felt betrayed.

But how far my actions were removed from Yours, Lord. Where You were filled with pity, I was intensely angry. I remember saying, "This is incredible. It's the last straw." How furious I was as I drove away from the house en route to noon Mass. Then You had pity on me. You made me think of the parallel of Your betrayal and say to myself: "Is this how you imitate your Lord in your little holy week?" You, Lord, washed the feet of Judas, I just wanted to wash my "betrayer" out of my life.

Even though I remained hurt and angry so that I found it difficult to keep my mind on the Mass, I remember thinking of your words, "If you have anything against your brother when you come to offer sacrifice, leave the sacrifice at the altar, go first and be reconciled to your brother and then come and offer your gift." In my mind I did make peace and say that I forgave, and I offered some of my prayers during Mass and after Holy Communion for the perpetrator of this scheme that had so upset me; but I didn't do it very well. I had to keep repeating it all because angry thoughts continued to crowd into my mind. I believe I forced the spirit to be willing but the flesh remained abysmally weak. Now, Lord, days later, I again reaffirm my forgiveness and my desire to forget and my hope that we will remain or come again to be friends.

It appears that Wednesday of Your Holy Week, Lord, was for You a day of rest. It was not quite that way for me. After being admitted to the hospital I had to go through a battery of tests; then I was assigned to a room that I shared with an engaging gentleman who was soon to be discharged. We had much in common; he, too, was a long-time employee of the federal government and was nearing retirement. We shared many exchanges about our respective adventures in working for Uncle Sam.

A dedicated Lutheran, he told me some of his experiences with his fellow believers and I explained to him what I had been doing as a permanent deacon for the past four years. Ours was an ecumenical room.

Kathleen stayed most of the afternoon, helping to make me comfortable, and strolling with me down the corridor to the solarium where we sat and visited, being interrupted from time to time by nurses, interns, and resident doctors who wanted to get acquainted, conduct interviews, and perform additional tests.

Even so it was a kind of day of rest, though far different, Lord, from Yours at the home of Mary, Martha, and Lazarus in Bethany near Jerusalem.

On Thursday I had planned to spend as much time as possible reading about and meditating on Your Holy Thursday: how You went into Jerusalem to have the feast with Your chosen ones, sending Peter and John to make the arrangements for the guest chamber where they were to prepare the Passover; Your washing the feet of your disciples, even those of Judas; how You answered the questions of Thomas, Philip, Jude, and Peter. And the Last Supper of Your mortal life, with the institution of the blessed Eucharist, followed by Your touching discourse in which You emphasized so often that the sign of apostleship would be love for one another. Your giving the new commandment that Your disciples should love one another as You loved them; and of course, Your priestly prayer to Your Father asking for unity, oneness, among Your followers.

My intentions to read and meditate on all this, as well as on Your agony in Gethsemane, were good; but I found little opportunity that day. In addition to having more tests, x-rays, and interviews, I wished to spend as much time as possible with Kathleen. Also, my roommate wanted to talk and I thought that here was another opportunity to practice the little way by doing what pleased him rather than me.

I did receive You in Holy Communion, Lord, sometime after the end of visiting hours, perhaps at about the time of evening when You instituted the Eucharist. Normally I could have meditated at length, but a sleeping pill or sedation of some sort had been prescribed and I dozed off.

How very different were my Holy Thursday night and Good Friday from Yours, Lord. You endured Your agony in the solitude of the garden. *I, like Peter, James, and John, fell fast asleep.*

You were seized by Your enemies and your friends ran away. *I was surrounded by persons intent on taking care of me.*

You were hailed before Annas and then Caiphas and the Sanhedrin, falsely accused, struck by a servant, reprehensibly condemned for telling the truth about Yourself, and denied three times by the one whom You had chosen as the rock of

Your community of believers. *No one accused me of anything, no one rejected me.*

In the morning they brought You before Pilate who sent You to Herod who sent You back to Pilate. *I got up and shaved.*

You were scourged and a crown of thorns was driven into Your scalp. *I was given a sedative.*

Whereas Your people cried out "Crucify, crucify" until Pilate condemned You to death, *preparations were made to save me from disease and restore me fully to health.*

The soldiers laid on Your shoulders one of the timbers to which You were to be nailed. They drove You through the streets like an animal, so that You fell again and again under the weight of the timber and Your immense weariness, tearing Your knees open on the rough stones, every part of Your body throbbing with pain as You collapsed to the ground. *The attendants came to my room, placed me on a stretcher, and wheeled me away.*

You met Your Mother on the way to Your brutal death. *Kathleen walked down the hall alongside the stretcher, held my hand and kissed me and we said, "I love you."*

You climbed a hill, with every step sheer torture. *I rode down three floors in an elevator.*

When You arrived on Golgotha they stripped You naked, tearing open all Your wounds. *When I reached the operating room they made sure I was as warm and comfortable as possible.*

Your executioners offered You wine mixed with gall to ease the pain of Your coming crucifixion. You refused it. *An anesthetist introduced herself to me and then after a little while said, "In just a few seconds you will go to sleep."*

They hammered spikes through Your wrists and feet and You prayed, "Father, forgive them." *The surgeon's knife cut into my flesh and I felt nothing.*

For three hours You hung in agony on the cross choking to death. Every time You spoke, leaving us messages of love, You had to push your bleeding hands and feet against the iron nails to get air into Your lungs. You endured all the pains of a body that was despoiled, brutalized, tortured beyond my ability to conceive of it. *I experienced not one twinge.*

Your blood ran down the wood of the cross and down Your body, falling to the ground. *I bled, too, but they gave me three pints of someone else's blood to replace what I had lost.*

They took You down from the cross and laid Your lifeless body in a tomb. *They took me, still asleep, to a recovery room and then to my own room.*

Oh, what a difference, dear Lord, between Your Thursday and Good Friday and mine. I bore at most a sliver of Your cross of suffering; You bore all of mine except a sliver.

And yet our Thursdays and Fridays are joined by the action of our wills. You offered Yours for me: I offered mine to You. Therefore they are one.

But is it really true? Can events so different yet be one?

During Your Passion all the powers of evil were concentrated against You. Satan hurled at You every horror of which he was capable, wracking Your soul, torturing Your mind, wringing You out, seeking to drain You of strength and energy and all that would bring You even a shred of peace and consolation. Evil personified encased You in a chamber of horrors, determined to break Your human will, to cause You to say, "No, Father, *my* will, not yours, be done!"

You were surrounded by hatred. I was surrounded by love.

In Your Passion, good and evil were locked in combat as never before or since. What it cost You to win! What a price, what an agony! Is it really true that my little passion could be united to Yours?

Satan lost his battle with You, Lord, but he won against almost everyone else. He could not win over You; but he won over Judas. How he led and twisted and deceived him so that he conspired to sell You and brought the enemy to You and betrayed You with a kiss. How successfully Satan turned the remorse of Judas into despair so that he hanged himself.

He won against the apostles, scattering them so that they ran like frightened rabbits fleeing for safety in the dark night.

How completely he won over Peter. This man, chosen to be the chief of your apostles and head of your Church, swore to Yahweh that he had never laid eyes on You.

Satan could not get inside of You; but how well he succeeded in getting inside of Your tormentors. You were no ordinary man, no common criminal; they could see that. There was about You an aura of goodness and gentleness and immense courage. But Satan got inside of them and stirred them to utter fury when they could not break Your spirit, make You scream, force You to beg. So they flogged You until they were exhausted.

Satan could not tell You what to do. But how skillfully he manipulated Caiphas and Annas and the chief priests and elders of the Law—so that they rejected the very Law itself and the need for witnesses whose testimony agreed in their evil determination to kill "one man for the good of the whole nation."

Satan could not make a coward of You; but how thoroughly he cowed Pilate. He pinned him to the wall as though he were a fly; and Pilate squirmed and wriggled and twisted to get out of condemning an innocent man, but finally gave in because of fear of what the Jewish leaders would report to Rome.

What a night and day of sin that was; surely the worst that has ever been.

Yet there were a few whose love resisted the onslaught of evil: Mary, Your Mother, and her sister, the wife of Cleophas, and the Magdelan, and John who had come back to watch You die. Yes, and Peter who was now weeping bitterly but who lacked the courage to come to Calvary, perhaps because he could not bear to have You look at him again. But above all, there You were Lord, giving all of Yourself. Love on that day conquered evil forever. You were, as Paul wrote, God's "yes," the answer to all God's promises.

Can it be that Thursday night while I slept and my Friday when I lay insensible can be joined to Yours by an act of my will? You say it, Lord. It must be so.

You did not let Satan come near me. You did not permit me to be tried even a little, no doubt because You know how weak I am.

Yet with Paul, I believe that I have a share in Your many sufferings. With him, I offer myself to You, "a living sacrifice dedicated and fit" for Your acceptance, "the worship offered by mind and heart."

With Paul, I can say, "All I want is to know Christ . . . to share in his suffering and become like him in his death, in the hope that I myself will be raised from death to life."

Chapter Five

Resurrection

I remember nothing of the rest of my Friday and not a great deal of Saturday. On Sunday, however, I had a kind of resurrection in that I was fully conscious again and feeling quite comfortable.

There was also a deeper parallel. On Your day of Resurrection, You emerged from the tomb, Your body glorified, as glorious indeed as You are in heaven at the right hand of Your Father. On my day of resurrection, which was not Easter but, so appropriately, the feast of Corpus Christi, You came to me—the same glorified Christ—and I took You on my tongue and You penetrated to the very core of my being to continue Your work of transforming me into You.

You made my convalescence easy, Lord, but then You do such things so often. You present us with an impending trial and when we accept it the trial dissolves like a dream. As You know I had some discomfort, but not much real pain, except for one short burst of near agony when an orderly removed the dried blood that had formed around the catheter on the most sensitive part of my body. I'm sure he had no idea how much he was hurting me, or if he did he undoubtedly felt that he had to push to its conclusion the work he was doing. The pain, however, was truly almost unbearable and I remember praying, "Oh, God, let him stop. Make him stop." But my will was also saying, "I would not change it, Lord, I would not change it—only help me to bear it."

Such discomfort as I had from the numerous drawings of blood, the injections, and all that goes on in preoperative and postoperative care were easily borne. Every time they took blood, I remember saying inwardly, "I give this blood to You, my Lord, in exchange for the blood You shed for me."

Such small offerings on my part to be joined to such a magnificent totality of oblation on Yours!

There was only one time when it seemed that the trouble I had feared and that had occurred after the operation on my eye might be about to recur. A few days after surgery I began to vomit, and after it happened three times on one day there was some uneasiness on the doctor's part that a chain reaction might develop, but it did not.

To help prevent it, and because I was low on blood, the doctor ordered a transfusion of two more units of blood. This was four days after the operation. The first unit entered my vein rather well, but shortly after the second unit was begun the flow became slower and slower and a numbness developed in my lower arm. After a while my whole arm became numb and pressure in my chest made breathing somewhat difficult. Though I was lying flat, my pulse shot up to 120 beats per minute. At that point I turned on the light to call the nurse. She came in, looked at me, summoned the head nurse and soon several nurses were standing around taking my pulse, listening to my heart through a stethoscope, and asking me about the tightness in my chest.

I thought I might be about to have a heart attack, but I was not really alarmed. I recall thinking, "Maybe now You are going to let me suffer a little." I remember being amused by the way the nurses kept their air of calm so long as they were in the room and I could see them; but the moment one of them left, my eye caught a flare of skirts as she began to run as quietly as she could down the corridor. Then there were calls for Dr. so-and-so.

A nurse came in with another apparatus for taking blood pressure. Although they had already done it twice, apparently they were not satisfied.

Then word came that the blood transfusion was to be discontinued but that the saline solution should go on until the bottle was empty.

What the problem was You know, Lord, and I assume the doctors do also. All I know is that after a while my breathing became easier and the numbness in my chest and arm disappeared. To ascertain whether damage had been done, however, another electrocardiogram was taken; so far as I am aware it proved to be all right.

That was about all the excitement I had, Lord. You were certainly easy on me.

I keep asking myself: Do I dare to conclude, Lord, that this week of mine was indeed a holy week? I think it was. I gave You my will, as totally, I believe, as I was capable of doing at the time. I wanted what You wanted—no more, no less. As I look back over these weeks preceding and following my surgery, in particular my holy week itself, they seem to have been spiritually the most joyful of my entire life.

How good You are, how loving, how munificently You repay us for our willingness to do some tiny thing for You.

You know, my dear Lord, that in speaking about prayer I have often relied on what some of the Fathers of the early Church have said or implied, namely that You made in our name such a sacrifice, that You put your Father in our debt. I have often used this thought in homilies on prayer, pointing out that Your promise that whatever we should ask the Father in Your name He would grant was based upon Your sacrifice in our name; that Your sufferings, obedience, and love have an infinite value that makes the eternal Father owe us; therefore even if it were possible for the Father to refuse us anything as Father, whatever we ask in Your name and with our wills united to Yours He cannot in justice refuse. He must hear our prayer in the way that is best.

This, dear Lord, is a teaching that for some years has meant much to me. Now, however, it has come to mean immeasurably more. Now You permit me to feel that Your expression of limitless love is not just Yours but mine also. You permit me to feel that I hung on the cross with You, that I have given my blood and my love with You. My flesh has been pierced, only so little it is true, but pierced nevertheless along with Your flesh. Spiritually I have died with You, spiritually I have been resurrected with You.

Because I have given You as best I could, my willingness to endure whatever you might permit, Your Passion and my passion have truly become one in Your eternal and all-knowing vision. My insignificant sacrifice was all that You wanted of me at this time. How sweet is Your yoke, how light the burden You lay on us!

Now, Lord, where do I go from here? I have made a kind of month-long retreat under Your direction. I know that You direct every retreat; all our good thoughts and impulses, our insights and lights come from You and Your Holy Spirit. But in a special way, Lord, I have felt that You were indeed my retreat master during these weeks. In the words of Ezekiel, You have given me a new heart, put a new spirit in me, removed the heart of stone from my body and given me a heart of flesh instead.

How shall I continue? Or rather, what shall I do to let You continue the work that You have begun? Of myself all I can do is hinder You and get in Your way. I have been living in a spiritual hothouse. In the hospital I was singularly blessed by the many priests who seemed almost to vie with one another in their desire to bring You to me in Your blessed Eucharist. Since I've been home I have still been living in a spiritual hothouse, protected against the temptations, problems, and irritations that come to all of us as we go about our work.

I know from experience how easy it is to gradually slip from a spiritual height and begin to slide and tumble and fall as though down a hillside, then to reach a stopping point and look back up the hill to see how far and how quickly I have fallen.

I'm not asking, Lord, and You know this is true, for any continued consolations or feelings of Your presence. I believe You taught me long ago the importance of simply living by faith, accepting from Your Hand whatever You send, gladdening or less gladdening, an oasis or a desert, though I'm sure the deserts in which You have permitted me to wander have not been real deserts at all but only little arid places. What I ask is not to be consoled or enlightened, but simply that You help me so that rather than refusing or misusing the immensely wonderful gifts of grace, faith, and trust that You have bestowed on me in these weeks, I may always keep my face and my heart turned toward You. Help me to grow in You precisely as You wish me to.

This retreat with You seems to me to be in a very small way akin to Paul's retreat in the desert where You taught and formed him and gave him insights that changed his life. Am I going to be changed when I go again into the world? Or will all this prove to be just a quickly forgotten dream? Not that I am in any realistic sense another Paul or even that I would want to be because, again like Philip Neri, I feel like saying to You, "Beware of me, lest I betray You."

I guess what I am asking, Lord, is how shall I know how to live as You wish me to? When I go back to my work again, I know I will be subject to the distractions, appeals to vanity and ambition, the urges to put myself forward that I have encountered before. The world encourages us to be self-seeking, and You know, Lord, how competitive I am, how I desire to excel, to come in first in whatever I undertake. You know how large a factor this competitiveness has been in my life. Because I have had a crippling stammer for most of my life, I was driven to become a public speaker. I could not rest from seeking to develop the ability to speak, and speak well, which for so long had been impossible.

You know that in my writing I have consistently refused to let go of a book or an article until I was satisfied that I could do no better. You know how hard I have tried to excel not only at work but at games like chess, bridge, tennis, and how doggedly I would seek out the hardest puzzles and refuse to concede defeat, wasting hours in such almost fruitless contests.

Much of this has been ameliorated, Lord, in recent years; yet I know that latent in me is still this burning desire to excel—for my own sake and my own satisfaction.

Teach me as You did Paul to distrust myself and depend solely on You. This was a hard lesson for Paul as it is for everyone, and as it must be for me.

It would have been natural and easy for Paul to have tried to preach Your message with an orator's cleverness. But he did not. He deliberately obscured any talent of that nature that he possessed and concentrated simply on talking about You, Christ crucified and Christ risen. Rather than using the phrases of polished orators, employing debaters' tricks, or scouring his mind for humanly effective ways to present Your message, he simply threw it at people with all the force of his vibrant personality.

Paul learned that his strength was his weakness and that when he most acknowledged his weakness, then he was strongest with Your strength.

I beg You to help me learn this lesson thoroughly, even as You have helped me begin to learn it during these weeks. Help me to imitate Thérèsè and like her to glory in being inconspicuous, small, and overlooked. I feel, Lord, that all I desire now is to be inconspicuous for You, to be passed over and ignored, to seek no honor, no place, no prestige. Yet I wonder whether this is just a coat of paint that You have permitted to cover my natural inclinations. How long will I cling to this desire? How long before I begin again to envy others their skills rather than rejoicing in their use of them for You? How long before I begin to say proudly and competitively as I have so often, "I can do better than that. I can do better than he?" How long before what I begin as Your work again becomes primarily my work?

When I think of the allurements of ambition to which I will soon again be subjected, I wonder how I shall keep alive the lessons You have taught me.

But I have confidence in You, Lord. I place all my trust in You. Only be especially careful of me, I beg You, so that I may not give way. Help me to seek to be the least for Your love. Help me to take no pride in any homily I may preach, any words I may write, any achievement I may accomplish.

Let me realize, Lord, that all success comes from You and give all glory to You.

Make me able to say with the psalmist: "O Lord, my heart is not proud nor haughty my eyes. I have not gone after things too great, nor marvels beyond me.

"Truly I have set my soul in peace and silence. As a child has rest in its mother's arms, even so my soul."

Chapter Six

Let Every Drop of Water Give You Glory

Lord, I have shown what I have written to a few persons whose knowledge and judgment I respect, and they have all expressed the hope that it will be published. But they also all agree that something more is needed, specifically some explanation of how the close relationship that exists between us came to be, or more accurately how I came to recognize, appreciate, and understand this relationship.

I hesitate to reveal Your kindness in bringing me closer and closer to You so that I feel free to talk to You as I have in these pages. Do You want me to reveal this? Truly, I cringe at the prospect of laying bare what I have come to realize are immense favors. Moreover, self-revelation poses danger for me because it can so easily slide into self-glorification.

Still, in a way that I cannot quite fathom, I am compelled to go on recording my thoughts and conversations with You even though I come back again and again to that statement of Francis's about the grace to conceal a grace.

My advisors say that relating what I have experienced may help some who seek to know You better, some who are encountering problems and crosses, some who are beset by fear, even by dread, and this seems reasonable. So I shall follow their advice and will talk with You about how You have blessed me throughout my life, enabling me to know and love You, to feel at home with You, to speak to You not only as creature to Creator but as friend to friend and brother to brother. What is to be done with these reflections, however, You must decide.

The first recollection I have, Lord, of being attracted to a very intimate relationship with You revolves around an incident that occurred when I was ten or eleven and in the fifth or sixth grade. Toward the end of Lent that year I saw a play presented by the dramatic club of my parish, the title of which I've long since forgotten although I recall that it was about You and Your sufferings. Suddenly a thought strikes me: Could it have been *The Upper Room*? In any event, after seeing it once, I could hardly wait to go back for another performance; it spoke to me about You in terms I had never before experienced.

It was on the afternoon of the Sunday before Easter that I returned for the second showing, sitting rapt and oblivious to all except the action on the stage. I came out of the playhouse to a cloudy, raw March afternoon and almost in a daze walked the block to our parish church. I wanted to pray, wanted to be with You. Three or four adults were in the church and I remember being encouraged by their presence because I had a strange feeling about what I was doing. I went to a front pew, fell on my knees, gazed at the tabernacle and began speaking to You in my own words.

There was a stillness in the church, the only sounds being the rustle of clothing when one of the worshippers changed position. After a while I was no longer conscious even of those noises. The cloudy day provided a gray light through the stained glass windows, but the many votive candles and the sanctuary lamp blinked and flickered cheerfully. I felt *right*. I seemed to know that some aspect of life was opening for me, something new, unexplored, and first. I had a realization of how much You loved me and it was startling, satisfying, exhilarating, and awe-full.

How long I remained there, looking at You behind the tabernacle door and after a while not even whispering to You but just being *with* You, telling You wordlessly how grateful I was and how I did indeed love You also, I do not know—but it was surely a long time for a youngster, perhaps more than an hour, and no one remained in the church when I left.

Walking home I felt transported, carried out of myself, so that I looked at the people I met and the houses, trees, grass, the sky, and the world in a way that was new to my youthful eyes.

Throughout the rest of Holy Week, I continued to feel Your presence. I was happy, recollected, absorbed; nothing was so easy or so satisfying as praying and thinking about You. On Holy Thursday I went to morning Mass, made a visit in the afternoon and returned again for Holy Hour in the evening. From somewhere I had acquired a set of really beautiful holy cards, much larger than the ordinary, and of quite good artistic quality, one showing You at prayer in the garden, others depicting some of Your miracles, and one or two of the crucifixion. I remember sitting on a chair in a corner of the dining room studying the pictures, and thinking about what they represented.

After a while I got up, moved over beside my mother or my favorite aunt, who were both in the dining room, and showed them the holy cards. "Aren't these pictures beautiful?" I asked shyly, because I knew I was revealing something about myself that I wasn't sure I wanted to and I didn't know how they would react. Whoever it was that I spoke to took the cards, looked at them one by one, not hurriedly the way older persons sometimes do when a child shows them something, then looked at me in a kind of surprise, and finally replied quietly, "Yes, they are very beautiful." I went back to my chair with a peculiar sense of satisfaction.

Those days, I realize now, must have been a time of munificent graces for me; but then, of course, I didn't understand. I just knew that I was caught up in an awareness of You and a relationship with You, Lord, that I had not had before.

It goes without saying that after this experience I was never again the same person; how could I be? My awareness of You ebbed and flowed, but it never became so dissipated that I totally lost what You had given me. Baseball season came, along with summer-time, and I was caught up as before in the delight of the solid hit, the spectacular catch, the good curve, and getting a measure of control over the fast ball. But I also prayed more, and thought more about You, and stayed after morning Mass, and dropped into church from time to time during the day to visit with You.

Looking back over my life, Lord, I recognize that You gave me special spiritual nourishment as I needed it. There must have been continual calls, but some stand out in memory. You would raise me to a spiritual height of some sort; then the ebb and flow would set in until there came a time when I was drifting too far, and You would bring me back in some special manner. No doubt, Lord, I failed to respond many times, and surely there must have been many spiritual touches that I no longer recollect when I shut the door on You or opened it only a little or in various ways turned my back on You.

An experience that I do remember rather clearly occurred during my first year of high school at Columbia Academy in Dubuque, Iowa. Our religion class was studying the Gospel according to Luke under Father William Russell, who had a unique capacity to bring the gospel to life even in the resisting and restless minds of fourteen- and fifteen-year-old boys. On this occasion Father Russell took the sentence, "And Jesus steadfastly set his face to go to Jerusalem," and drew out of the phrase "steadfastly set his face" a vivid and unforgettable lesson in courage. Many times in my life, as You know, Lord, when I wanted to run away from challenges and difficulties, I recalled how You steadfastly set Your face to go to Your suffering and death, and I found in Your example the courage and strength I needed. It was the Holy Spirit's gift of fortitude.

Good psychologist that he was, Father Russell understood that to boys of our age, courage was the quality we most admired. He helped me to see You, Lord, in Your human dimensions. I recall word for word the question he put to us: "Did Jesus have guts?" A half-century ago the expression meant more than it does today. In our boys' vocabulary to have guts was to possess courage in all its facets: physical, moral, mental; to have optimism, stoicism, boldness, strength, equanimity, perseverance; it was more than courage; when uttered in praise it was about the highest accolade we could bestow. The mental picture I had of You, Lord, as a man of "guts" made You so visible I could almost literally see You striding steadfastly the path Your Father bade You walk, and setting Your teeth and jaw to confront those who would repudiate, condemn, torture, and crucify You.

My heightened awareness came at a strategically important time because I was beginning to run into a stormy period of my life. My stammer had become so acute that I could not recite in class or even respond to roll call. Answering the telephone or making a telephone call was next to impossible, largely because one day when I was alone I had forced myself to try to answer the telephone when someone was calling my father long distance. Because I could not speak intelligibly, the gentleman on the other end of the line, not understanding my problem and probably concluding that I was pretending to be unable to talk, cursed me terribly and left me with an emotional wound the scar of which has never completely faded. (Forgive him, Lord, for the hurt he inflicted on me, and forgive me also for the harm I have done to others.) I found it hard to talk to anyone except my closest friends who didn't care whether I stammered. As a result, I withdrew into myself until I became in many ways a confirmed introvert.

In addition, I was having the problems common to boys of my age with sexual temptations. Because of my stammer, going to confession became increasingly difficult. The upshot of all these intermingling circumstances was that I became scrupulous, and I don't suppose there is a worse time to acquire a pronounced case of scruples than when you are a boy of fourteen or fifteen. Nothing prepares you for it and you are too shy to ask for help, especially if you can't talk as was my situation.

I did much praying, much reading, and much thinking at this time. I was addicted to far too much introspection.

Something impelled me to write a paper, the gist being that if only people understood how much You loved them, Lord, they could not possibly offend You deliberately and could never turn their backs on You. I must have done this with the intention of giving it to Father Russell because I finished it one night and the next day I went to his room during the afternoon and slipped the paper, which was several pages, under his door. I must have felt keenly the need to love You myself and to help others to love You.

What I expected Father Russell to do with the paper, I have no idea. Probably I merely wanted to share it with him since he was the human instrument who had inspired it through his teaching. At the same time it was not easy to share it, especially for one who had become introverted. I had to "steadfastly set my own face" because while I believed You wanted me to do this, I shrank from doing it. Not that I feared a rebuff—I knew Father Russell could not be guilty of that—but I did not want to open myself to misunderstanding. To this day I can still almost feel the beating of my heart as I rapped timidly at his door, more than half hoping he would be out, holding my breath as I listened for his footsteps. Hearing nothing, I made myself knock again and wait before walking down the corridor with mingled relief and uneasiness, relief that he wasn't in and I would not have to explain what I was about. Relief and uneasiness because no sooner had I slid my paper under his door than I wanted it back. I had the same sense of unease and puzzlement about what I should do that I am experiencing now with respect to these reflections. How would he react? What would he think of me? Perhaps I had laid myself open to grave embarrassment.

Overnight my uneasiness deepened so that when I came to school the next day I hoped I wouldn't run into him, and if I did that he would ignore me. Between classes that morning we passed in the hall. He looked at me quizzically, nodded, smiled, and called me by name, but nothing more. It is obvious to me now that he was perceptive enough to recognize that I would have ambivalent feelings about what I had done.

Later that day we met again in the hall, and, since no one was within earshot, he stopped me and asked, "Why did you write that paper?" Father Russell had deep-set, piercing eyes and his gaze bored into me.

I replied in my halting way, "I don't know. I just felt that I wanted to say that if only we knew what Jesus had done for us, we couldn't act as we do. We wouldn't be mean anymore, maybe we wouldn't even have to be afraid of one another any-more." Probably it took five times as long for me to get this out as it has taken to type it. He waited for me to continue, but seeing that I had nothing more to offer, he nodded after a moment and said, "I see. Thank you very much for letting me read it. I think you're right. Would you like to have it back?"

I said, "No," and walked away, glad to close the incident. I had no copy of my paper and I never saw it again, and neither of us ever mentioned it although we came to know each other very well, especially when we both went on to the Catholic University of America in Washington, DC, he to teach and I as a graduate student. I don't believe he ever forgot the inci-dent, however. Obviously, I did not.

Another somewhat extraordinary event involving our deepening relationship, Lord, occurred in my senior year at the academy. An annual retreat was offered to the students beginning on Wednesday night of Holy Week and closing on Easter Sunday morning. It was a strict retreat with everyone staying at the school for the three-and-one-half days observ-ing silence. Since I was a day student and the retreats were optional, I had previously spent Holy Week in my parish. This retreat, then, conducted by two Jesuit fathers, was my first experience both with Jesuits and with retreats, and my expec-tation was heightened by what my older brothers and others had told me about the remarkable capabilities of the Jesuits and the equally remarkable effect the retreat would have on me. As You know, it was a very profitable event for me, Lord, and during it I prayed, read, and meditated and drew closer to You.

The retreat had such an effect that I was deliriously happy on Easter Sunday morning after the closing Mass and a hearty breakfast as I walked the mile or so down the hill toward my home. I knew again, Lord, as I had known after that first experience when I was ten or eleven what walking on air meant. I remember offering You everything, not only my voluntary thoughts, words, and actions, but every beat of my heart, every breath I took. In physics class I had learned a little about the atom and I offered You the motion of every atom of my being. I looked heavenward and said, "I praise You with every particle of myself. I want to thank You and love You with all of my being." It was a kind of psalm of my own making, and the first time that I had ever done this. So far as I am aware, I had no realization of the psalms at that time, but I know now that this was a true psalm, a paean of praise and thanksgiving.

My consciousness of Your presence endured all that day and for several days thereafter. There was no need to think about You, I felt You there with me, and I simply rested in this knowledge. Although I was ignorant of the expression "prayer of quiet" and its meaning until many years later, I realize now that this was indeed the prayer of quiet and probably not the first time You had bestowed it on me. The first time, perhaps, was when I was in the fifth or sixth grade; my recollections of that earlier period, however, are dimmer and more likely to be confused.

During my senior year of college, in the heart of the Great Depression of the 1930s, I was trying to decide what to do with my life. I was still going to Columbia, which, like many private schools of that era, had both a high school and a college with separate buildings and faculty and almost a separate campus. Though it was not a prep seminary but a liberal arts college, Columbia for many years had enjoyed an enviable record of preparing young men for the priesthood.

As You know, Lord, I had often thought about becoming a priest, but I was also interested in a very attractive young lady.

During Holy Week—so many of my memories are associated with Holy Week—I made the second retreat of my life. For reasons beyond recall, I had passed up the opportunity to make the college retreat during my first three years just as I had done when in the academy. Because I was soon to be graduated and the problem of what to do after college pressed heavily upon me, I wanted to participate in this retreat in the hope that three days of prayer and silence would produce a solution. Since I truly wished to follow Your will, Lord, it was natural to wonder if You were asking me to be one of your priests. But I was in love.

Had I not been in love, I think I would have had little difficulty in seeing that the priesthood was not for me. But being torn between two strong attractions, I could not think straight. During the retreat I prayed most earnestly that You would help me find the answer.

There was an area of the campus known as Keane Oaks, named after an archbishop of the diocese, a large, secluded wooded tract where retreatants were accustomed to walk, pray, and meditate during the free hours. I walked in Keane Oaks on Friday from after the 3 o'clock Way of the Cross until dinner time, but I came no nearer to knowing what to do and in some ways seemed to be even more confused.

On Saturday both in the morning and again in the afternoon, I retired again to Keane Oaks alternately praying and thinking in a kind of desperate forced concentration, willing my mind to come up with a solution.

You know, Lord, that one of the factors involved in the decision was whether because of my stammer I had the physical qualifications to be a priest. If I could not recite in class, how could I expect to speak as a priest must? But for the fact that I was so much in love the answer would have been clear much sooner, but because my natural inclinations were urging me toward marriage, I feared that my stammer was only an excuse I was employing to justify my saying "no" to You.

Suddenly, after walking until I was tired to near exhaustion, too fatigued indeed to think or pray longer, I realized with an almost absolute certainty that I was not called to the priesthood. How could I preach? How could I give counsel in or out of the confessional? How could I read the prayers at Mass, confer the sacraments, comfort the sick, give solace to the bereaved? If You wanted me to be a priest at that time, I suddenly realized, You would have found a way to remove this speech handicap.

No sooner had the problem that had vexed me for so long been resolved that I wanted to leap into the air, click my heels, shout hooray—but I was too tired. Not too tired, however, to thank You. What a weight had been lifted! How profoundly grateful I was!

I recall returning home on Easter Sunday as I had after the high school retreat with complete lightheartedness. Again I found myself repeating my psalm, offering You every breath, every heartbeat, every movement of every atom, every particle of my being.

While it is impossible for me to remember all that was in my prayer on that Easter morning, I know that I praised You in and through all of creation. I praised You through the sun that You had made; I heard a dog barking and I praised you; I praised You through trees and grass and flowers; I saw the Mississippi River gleaming in the sunlight a couple of miles away and I breathed, "Let every drop of water give You glory, Lord."

That kind of prayer had been growing in me for years, Lord, and it has continued to grow up to the present day.

In my spiritual notes the other day I found the following reflections written a few years ago. They are presented as though You were speaking to me, Lord.

"When in your prayer you offer yourself to Me, do not be content with this alone. Offer Me everything! Do you know what I mean by this?

"First, I would have you offer Me all that you think, say, or do. This, of course, you already know; it is obvious that you would offer Me all that is voluntary.

"But I desire more. Offer Me also everything that is involuntary, every beat of your heart, every movement of your muscles, every blinking of your eyelids, every motion in and of every atom of your body.

"And still I desire more. Offer Me the glory of all creation. You can do this because you are part of the family of creation. Offer Me, then, the glory of this family of which you are one member—the glory given to Me by the dog wagging its tail or barking its warning, by the horse, the cow, the bird, the bee, the ant, the fish fulfilling their functions in My plan; the glory given Me by the tree, the blade of grass, the acorn, the leaf, the seed; the glory given to Me by the mountains and every stone that is in them, by the seas and every drop of water they contain, by the land and every grain of sand on the beach.

"But I desire still more. Offer Me all the glory that is Mine and that is owed to Me by the whole human family, by all your brothers and sisters over all the earth—in America, Europe, Asia, Africa, by farmers, factory workers, merchants, captains of industry, commerce and finance, by seamen, students, teachers, artists; offer Me all the good they do or have ever done; offer Me your good intentions to compensate for the bad they do or have done; offer Me your conscious intention for their unconscious neglect.

"But still I must have more. Offer Me the glory not only of all your brothers and sisters now living, but that which has been given Me and was owed Me by all those who once lived and are now in eternity; offer Me the great works of the minds of all the Aristotles, the Platos, the Virgils, the Shakespeares, the art of all the Michelangelos and Leonardos, the military genius of the Hannibals, the Alexanders, the Napoleons, the labor of all who built the pyramids, the vaulting cathedrals, the great dams, everything that man has ever done or thought or said. Offer Me the love of every mother nursing her baby at her breast, the love of every husband for his wife and wife for husband.

"And yet more! Still more! Offer Me the love of My saints. Offer Me My Mother's love, Joseph's love, Peter's love, John's love, Paul's love; offer Me all the devotion of Catherine, of Francis, of Teresa and Thérèsè, of Ignatius, and of the vast host of saints known and unknown who are one with the Trinity in heaven, and the homage of all who are this day in purgatory.

"And still I desire more! Offer to your God the very love of the Father for the Son and Son for the Father, the expression of which is the Holy Spirit, the Spirit of Love Himself.

"This is the sum of My desire, My other self; for I want you to pray not because I need it, but because you do. To offer this prayer is your privilege; an honor I have bestowed on you."

Something else of note occurred during my senior year. I encountered as fine a teacher as anyone could hope to meet. You know who I mean, Lord. John Flynn was a young diocesan priest who had taken his theological studies in Rome and then had studied philosophy at Louvain. He returned to teach at Columbia, possessing a doctorate in philosophy and advanced degrees in theology. John Flynn had one of those startlingly open Irish faces with an enthusiasm to match. How his countenance would light up whenever an idea struck fire!

He would come to class lugging five or six tomes that he would set on the desk before launching into his lecture on the history of philosophy. So far as I can remember he never once opened any of them in class, though he would hold them up as illustrative props while speaking about this or that philosopher. He used no notes. Ideas simply poured from his lips in a stream of golden eloquence. Like another John, he, too, might have been called "Chrysostom" because his eloquence, his thought, his personality, and his voice were all golden.

Obviously, he loved his subject. He spoke of it with wild bursts of enthusiasm, his eyes flashing and his hair thoroughly tousled and tangled because he ran his hand through it whenever a lock fell over his eyes.

I'm morally certain that he was conscious of almost nothing while he lectured except the ideas erupting in his mind and cascading in verbal form from his lips and of us, his students. He kept looking from one to another of us, boring into us with his eyes, his whole body lending itself to the excitement of his teaching. I could no more turn away from the flow of ideas that he seemed to be driving directly into my mind than I could stop a bullet emerging from the barrel of a rifle by holding up my hand.

For the first time, I became truly fired up about a school subject. Oh, I had been interested before, but not on fire with a throbbing eagerness to learn more and more and more. In my eagerness I read everything Father Flynn recommended to us on the history of philosophy and the philosophical systems, and I didn't stop with his list.

It paid dividends in the end-of-term examination. I remember writing as excitedly as Father Flynn had lectured, filling first one blue examination booklet and then another, and perhaps part of a third, my pen struggling to keep pace with my thoughts. I was the last student to leave the room and I walked down the hall mentally exhilarated and happy but with my hand aching from the constancy and speed of my writing.

When we returned to class the next week, I knew an embarrassing situation was developing almost as soon as Father Flynn began to speak about the examination. He said that he had received one paper that so far surpassed all the rest in knowledge, synthesis, and understanding, it was as though an advanced graduate student had written it. As soon as he cited a detail or two I was certain he was referring to my paper. I lowered my head, looked at the floor, and undoubtedly blushed to the roots of my hair. I wished he would stop, yet I relished what he was saying. I hoped, at least, that he would not mention my name—but he did.

I relate this, Lord, to pay tribute to one of Your servants for whom I had immense admiration and affection, and to whom I owe much. Outside of class we had not spoken twenty words to each other and we did not speak that day either. I was too embarrassed to do anything but hurry from the room as soon as we were dismissed. I knew that if I tried to speak I would stammer so badly I could only gabble. I regret that I never told John Flynn how much he inspired me. What a marvelous gift it is, Lord, to be able to open a youthful mind—and how brilliantly John Flynn used Your gift.

Why didn't I tell him? You know why, Lord. First, it was hard for me to speak to anyone, especially when I was under the stress of emotion. But I'm sure I would have eventually except for what happened very shortly.

For the second semester I had signed up for two philosophy classes under Father Flynn. The semester had hardly begun, however, when a substitute teacher came to class. Father Flynn, he told us, was in the hospital seriously ill from something that the doctors found difficult to diagnose. He asked us to pray. A couple of days later when he told us that John Flynn's condition was so critical the doctors held out little hope, I was crushed. It was impossible. I could not accept it. Yet as I discovered on further inquiry, it was all too true.

At that time my home parish, St. Mary's, the same church in which I had my first deep awareness of You some ten years earlier, was having its annual Forty Hours Devotion. On both Monday and Tuesday, after my last class, I walked down the hill and went directly to the church. I joined the rather large group of worshippers and prayed for a whole hour with them and well into a second hour. I asked You, Lord, to spare my friend, if it would be Your will. At night I returned for the evening devotions. After the close of the Forty Hours on Tuesday night, I remember feeling a kind of peace.

John Flynn died that week. Although desolate, I had faith enough to understand that he was with You, Lord, and that was immeasurably better than being with us.

Later, with my mother and father, I went to the wake. I wonder if it was largely because of me that they went. They knew the Flynn's but not at all intimately. I had never met any of Father's family, so I was surprised when one of his sisters came up and when we were introduced she said, "You're the one Father John talked about so much. He thought so very highly of you."

As we left the house and got into our car, her words remained. Do You remember, Lord, (how foolish! of course You do) that I resolved to do my best to make something of myself in memory of John Flynn?

Lord, as I review my life, I know that there were many times when I prayed very earnestly and very long; but this is one that stands out vividly, starkly, in human terms almost cruelly.

It was the first time that I had prayed to You with all of my heart, and all of my soul, and all of my mind, and all of my strength—and You said, "No!" You were teaching me something about abandonment, Lord. You were showing me what it really means to pray, "Your will, not mine, be done."

Again I ask, Lord, why am I doing this, what purpose can it serve? Wouldn't it be better to keep all this between us? How I wish I knew for sure what You desire. Am I repeating the experience of Keane Oaks so many years ago, and is the answer once again just beyond my comprehension, so clear once I see it, so opaque until the darkness is dispelled? Am I again so torn between two loves that I cannot think straight? The thought of revealing what I am writing to the cold eyes of everyone who might chance upon it repels me. But every time

I say to myself, "No more. This is it. I will file it away," I am drawn to continue by the possibility that You want me to go on. So I shall, trusting that You in Your own good time will make Your will clear to me as You did then.

Through many means You have brought me closer to You, my Lord. As is evident, priests have exercised a predominant influence on my life. At almost every turning a priest has helped provide advice, direction, guidance, and prayer; and not only at the turnings but throughout the course, on the straightaways so to speak, the influence of priests has been a persistent tonic. My oldest brother, whose example of obedience and generosity pervades his life, and our oldest son, also one of Your priests, who exhibits a remarkable devotion to serve You especially through youth, never fail to inspire me.

To mention even briefly what these and many other priests have done to awaken my love for You and for the Church would require a book in itself. But why should I try to tell You, Lord, what You already know far better than I? Let me simply thank You for what you have done for me through Your priests.

You also led me to You through books. I remember a prayer book entitled, I believe, *My Prayer Book,* written by a Father Lasance, which was popular when I was a boy. In the front section the author had compiled a large assortment of readings from spiritual writers, some old, some modern. There was an interesting passage on kindness written by Father Faber, an associate of Cardinal Newman, and another on the virtue of abandonment to the divine will, both of which I devoured over and over as was my custom when deeply impressed by anything I read. I would go over such passages before Mass and sometimes, I must confess, during the sermons.

Let me skip over the years, Lord, to the time when a zealous young priest who was stationed at the Apostolic Delegation in Washington, DC, entered our lives. Kathleen and I met him for the first time at a Cana Conference, became friends with him, and had the pleasure of having him become a regular visitor at our home. This was when Kathleen and I had been married about ten years and had a thriving young family.

Once or twice a week we would sit in the living room or around the dining room table sipping coffee and talking about the spiritual life until one or two in the morning. How many new vistas You opened for me in this way. It was during this period that I began two practices that became of paramount importance in my life. I began to read extensively on the spiritual life and on the saints, and I also began to make notes on the insights You were permitting me to have in prayer. It was largely out of these notes that the book *My Other Self* was constructed.

As for the reading: Henri Gheon's *Secrets of the Saints,* containing short sketches of the Cure d'Ars, Thérèsè, Margaret Mary, and John Bosco, opened my mind to the saints as real human beings rather than characters in a novel or play. Having relished Gheon's biographies, I began to read the writings of the saints themselves, among others Thérèsè's *Story of a Soul,* the *Introduction to the Devout Life* and the *Treatise on the*

Love of God by Francis de Sales, the works of Teresa of Avila, and those of John of the Cross. As a result I became increasingly interested in prayer and then in Father Jean-Pierre de Caussade's *Abandonment to Divine Providence* and his exposition of the "sacrament of the present moment."

I not only read about prayer, I prayed. There was a time, as You know, Lord, when I devoted three or four hours every day to prayer, somehow managing to spend this much time without taking anything away from my family or my work. Because of this experience I could write in Your Name in *My Other Self:*

> Give me of your time, and I will do half and more of your
> work,
> Give Me your thoughts, and I will enlighten your mind.
> Give Me your will, and I will return to you My peace.
> Give Me your love, and I will fill your days with joy.
> Give Me your prayers, and I will open to you the inex-
> haustible treasures of heaven.

Most of my prayer time was spent in wordless, silent, passive prayer. There came a time when I could not meditate any longer and fortunately I had read enough about progress in prayer to understand that one only meditates when one can. When you are unable to meditate, not so far as you can see for any fault of your own, you must then go on to other kinds of prayer as You, Lord, call us. The important thing is to accept, and will, and desire only the precise kind of prayer You permit us to have at any given moment.

More than once, Lord, as I knelt before You in the Blessed Sacrament, You gave me the strong, vivid realization of Your living presence in the host. You were there and I *knew* it. I could talk to You as Peter did. I could say, "Lord, it is good for me to be here." But far better than talking was just to kneel in Your presence—in the sunlight of Your real presence—and look at You with the clear gaze of faith. I asked You wordlessly what You would have me do. You answered that I should, as best I could, give You myself. And still, without a word being spoken, I replied that I wanted to do this, that I desired no merit, no reward, for myself, but only to love Your will.

It occurred to me to ask You to give me the great favor of always having this realization of Your presence. I started to ask, as You know, Lord, but then I stopped, and said to You that I wanted only Your will to be done, whatever it was.

Another time, Lord, again kneeling before the Blessed Sacrament, I was thinking that I did not want to see, but only to believe with all my self as I do believe. My eye fell on the crucifix—life-size—to the left of the altar—and I thought, "You could leave the tabernacle and enter that plaster figure, making it Yourself, and I could see You as You were hanging on the cross. I could see the huge spikes through Your wrists and through Your feet. I could see the flies buzzing about Your open wounds. I could see Your torn knees, blood-red and open, the countless lacerations on Your body, the dried blood and the running blood, the great welt on Your shoulder where the rough wood had crushed down upon You in Your many falls. I could see the thorns running into and through Your scalp, the puffed lips, the swollen nose, the battered, puffed brow swollen from the blows of Your tormentors. I could see Your tired Head slowly turn from side to side, like a heavy thing that You could move only by inches and with supreme effort."

And I knew, Lord, that even if I saw all this, You would not be as real to me on the cross as You were at that moment in the host; that I would turn my eyes from the cross and fix them on the host because that is where You really were. My human eyes could deceive me, but the eyes of faith could not.

Lord, what are You doing to me? I am getting deeper and deeper into a trackless forest. Worse, in a way, what I am writing will give readers a terribly false picture of me. Should anyone read this, I want him or her to realize that there has been immense ebb and flow in my spiritual growth, my prayer life, and my moral behavior. It seems that all I am setting down is the upside, the good side of the record, whereas You know, Lord, how large the downside bulks in the total story.

Yet I am not going to speak about the downside. Why? Because of pride? Maybe. But it is also a fact that the low points are not edifying and I cannot see how they could bring anyone to a better relationship with You. The downside of a person's life belongs in the confessional, put behind one, shed like a loose and useless skin. Whatever bad and whatever good I have done will be revealed on the last day and there will be no hiding it then. I pray with trust, Lord, that it will be made plain to my joy, not to my sorrow. There is no need now to track mud into the house. Just let anyone who sees this understand that there were low as well as high points. Where the balance is to be struck, Lord, only You know.

The writing of *My Other Self* was an important turning in my life. How can I thank You for the graces You showered on me, far more elaborate, far more abundant than I would ever have dared request. It is still something of a riddle to me how I happened to write that book. It came about in part because of our relationship with the young priest from the delegation. We used to talk about all the material written to help priests and religious grow in the spiritual dimension and about how little there was for the layperson. Since Francis de Sales's *Introduction to the Devout Life,* nothing of much note seemed to have been addressed to the spiritual needs of persons in the world.

Tired of hearing me grouse about this, our young friend asked, "Why don't you write something?" I said, "Don't be silly. I couldn't," and he replied, "How do you know?" I said, "Why me?" and he persisted, "Why not you?"

Forgive me for an outrageous comparison, but I can't help thinking of Yahweh and Moses. After Yahweh directs Moses to lead the Israelites out of Egypt, Yahweh, in answer to Moses's fears, promises Moses that He will be with him, will tell him what to say, and work signs and wonders for him. After all this, Moses still says, "If you please, Lord, send someone else." I felt exactly that way.

Nevertheless, I began to make copious notes based on the insights growing out of prayer, and after a while I began organizing these notes and putting them together in a readable form. Because I had long been talking with You as brother to brother, it seemed natural somehow to write *My Other Self* as though You were speaking to me and to be very intimate in expression as well as in thought.

I used what I had written as my own spiritual reading and as a springboard into the various kinds of prayer that You gave me. And I used it not once but dozens of times, adding a little here, deleting something there, until it finally came out as a book. You know, Lord, that there is far more of You in that book than there is of me. This, of course, is true of all of the good things that anyone does, but it was true in this instance in an extraordinary way.

Sometimes, Lord, when I go back to *My Other Self* now, I am bemused and puzzled and I ask myself, "Did I really write that? I don't remember it. Where did that thought come from?"

Is this true of writers generally, when they return to something they have composed years before, not only writers in the spiritual field but those in secular areas? I think perhaps it is, but I wonder if it can be true in the profusion of thought and the multiplication of ideas that seem so very strange to me when I read them now in *My Other Self.*

From time to time, Lord, I think of a little verse written by one of your priests early in this century.

WEAVING

My life is but a weaving
Between my God and me;
I may not choose the colors,
He knows what they should be;
For He can view the pattern
Upon the upper side,
While I can see it only,
On this, the underside.

Sometimes He weaveth sorrow,
Which seemeth strange to me;
But I will trust His judgement,
And work on faithfully;
'Tis He who fills the shuttle,
He knows just what is best;
So I shall weave in earnest
And leave Him with the rest.

At last, when life is ended,
With Him I shall abide,
Then I may view the pattern
Upon the upper side.
Then I shall know the reason

Why pain with joy entwined,
Was woven in the fabric
Of life that God entwined.

J.B. Tabb

I think of that verse and its application to my own life. I seem to feel Your hand, Lord, pushing me, prodding me, pulling me back, turning me in this direction or that, bringing me up short or speeding me along.

I began to see it more clearly than ever after I had become a permanent deacon. It is very evident to me now, Lord, that You meant me to be a permanent deacon from the beginning. You knew when You allowed me to realize almost half a century ago that I was not to be a priest, that someday I would be Your deacon. I marvel at the intricate inter-relationship of circumstances that made the diaconate possible for me.

First, there had to be an improvement in my ability to speak. This did not come about until I was in my late forties. I had learned to accept my stammering as a cross that You wanted me to carry, though You know, Lord, how long it was before I ceased to kick against the goad of this affliction. One night I mentioned this to the young priest from the delegation and he replied, "Maybe that's all the Lord wants of you, that you accept this, that you don't fight against it any longer. Maybe having accepted it, He wants you to begin now to try harder than ever to overcome it."

About that time, a set of circumstances began that did indeed lead me to achieve a great measure of control over my stammer. A friend in Baltimore, someone who really was not bound to me at that time in a very intimate friendship, took it on himself to arrange for me to attend a speech clinic in Baltimore. He made the calls to the director, he urged me to attend, and all I had to do was eventually say "yes" and then go. Although I had tried many other avenues of help before, it was at that speech clinic that I began to learn how to accept my stammering as a part of me and not to retreat from it or try to hide it, not to back off from speaking situations as I had done for decades. In this was the beginning of control.

A few years later another friend, again not one of my closest circle, introduced me to Toastmasters International. He urged me to come to a meeting with him and although I resisted, eventually I did go. After two Toastmaster meetings, one is expected to decide whether he wishes to become a member; but in view of my problem, I was permitted to attend more than the two meetings before deciding. I had great indecision about it, which was finally resolved, as You know, Lord, by my praying to You for guidance and then, when I was still unable to make up my mind, by simply tossing a coin with the understanding that if it came up "heads" I would join. It came up "heads" and the result was that I learned how to make prepared speeches before audiences of almost any size and to speak so fluently that hardly anyone hearing me for the first time would ever have known how badly I had been crippled by my stammer.

There were many problems, however, in other speaking situations. When I had to do something impromptu, I could not talk at all fluently even at Toastmasters. I had persistent and grave difficulties in conversation, and at times it was still almost impossible for me to speak over the telephone.

Obviously the basic difficulties that had steered me away from the priesthood still existed.

As a result of Vatican II, Your Holy Spirit led the Church during the 1960s to restore the order of the permanent diaconate. The first class of candidates in the Washington, DC, area went into training in 1969, and I was attracted strongly enough to the program to debate seriously applying for entrance. But the problems that remained with respect to conversation, telephoning, and reading aloud, though they had considerably ameliorated since I had come to accept my stammering and since I had learned to speak well in prepared situations, still seemed far too severe to enable me to carry out the responsibilities of the permanent diaconate. Consequently, I did not enter the first class.

Meantime, our oldest son was studying for the priesthood at Mt. St. Mary's Seminary in Emmitsburg, Maryland. The director of vocations for the Washington archdiocese began urging me to apply for admission to the diaconate program. I told him I did not think I was qualified physically. Although he accepted that for the moment, he came back to the subject often and finally he asked me, pointblank, "Don't you believe in the grace of orders?"—meaning, didn't I believe that You and Your Holy Spirit would supply the strength and the resources necessary, if it was Your will, that I should become a deacon?

I replied that I did indeed believe in the grace of orders. The upshot was that I entered the second class of candidates with the understanding that unless my speech problems cleared up sufficiently for me to function as a deacon I would not go through to ordination.

The course progressed with no noticeable improvement in my ability to speak. During the first year of training, since I had always been a past master at avoiding speaking situations and class recitations, I was able to survive without much difficulty. During the second year, the candidates began to give homilies. Thanks to Toastmasters, I had few problems with this. But the deacon candidates were also required to read passages from the Old and New Testaments at the Masses, and this I greatly feared I could not do.

I knew weeks in advance when I was scheduled to read and what the readings would be on that day. Realizing that this was, in a sense, the acid test, I practiced reading at home and at work. But I could not carry it off. Again and again and again I sought to train myself, trying by sheer repetition to force the words to flow fluently. All to no avail; indeed the more I practiced, the more I blocked. What were You telling me, Lord? Was it that unless You build the house, I labored in vain? My recollection is, Lord, that on the very day that I was to read, I could not, not only in Kathleen's presence but even to myself alone.

Well, You saw to it that I learned about the state of grace that night. I breathed a prayer to You and to the Holy Spirit and I asked my favorite saints to intercede for me, and then with a wildly beating heart I approached the lectern. Wonder of wonders, I read without a single speech block, without one verbal blemish. From that time as You know, Lord, I have had

no trouble reading the Word of God, and that is now almost
five years ago. I still have difficulties at times in reading the
announcements in church. Those are man's words, not God's.
Your words, Lord, as Shakespeare put it, lie trippingly on my
tongue.

Am I not correct then in thinking that in a special way You
marked me out as Your deacon?

*Clarence Enzler died unexpectedly on November 2, 1976. He
had been working on the second part of this book, which follows.
In part 2, he shifts from an accounting of his own spiritual life
to an encouragement for all to become saints. He was trying to
describe the aspirations and struggles of some of the saints and
offer suggestions for the spiritual life. This material had originally
been planned as a book by itself, but after he wrote his personal
account, he thought this should be added to it. He had intended
to put these chapters also in the same form of speaking intimately
to God.*

*As he described in the first chapters, Enzler was in great doubt
whether his personal spiritual journey should ever be published.
He asked God to make His will clear in this regard. Since his
own reluctance to bare all these inmost thoughts and his feelings
of presumption of the interest of others were the main reasons for
not publishing it, we took his death as that sign he had requested,
and decided on publication. As we did not want to change or add
anything, the second part may come abruptly upon the reader, but
we hope the author's intent will be clear.*

The Enzler Family

Part Two

Let Us Be
What We Are

Chapter Seven

All Are Called

God implants in every person the seed of greatness—the ambition to be somebody—the aspiration to heroism.

I like the way the late Father Edward Leen, C.S.Sp., put it in his work *In the Likeness of Christ*: Madeleine Sophie Barat, when she was told so often by her brother, a stern taskmaster, that she was worthless, resolved at least to be "great" in humility. And was this not why God inspired Thérèsè to follow her little way? She was unable to imitate the great feats of other saints, so she would at all costs be great in love.

And did not the soldier-noble pride of Ignatius lead him to ask himself whether he was "great" enough to compete with the saints in austerity and asceticism? He proved that he was.

Since God made us thus, it is not wrong for us to thirst for greatness. But how are our ambitions to be reconciled with God's commands not to seek the highest place, but the lowest; not to be served but to serve; not to receive but to give?

Clearly we must learn what God means by greatness. We must seek it where it truly exists and by God's means.

Where we fail is not only in misunderstanding the nature of greatness, but in remaining miserably ignorant of how great God has made us to be. To be His adopted sons and daughters—to be loved by Him as Jesus is loved; to possess His own life; to be *in* the eternal, omniscient, omnipotent God and *He in us*—what other greatness that we can conceive is even faintly comparable with this?

It is impossible to read the Gospels, the Acts, and epistles without feeling almost as a physical force the intensity with which the Lord desires all to be heroically great by being heroically holy. Speaking in His name, Paul in particular invited, exhorted, entreated, almost coerced his disciples to accept the goal of perfection.

"You must be clothed in a new self . . . sanctified through the truth," he told the Ephesians.

May the Lord "confirm your hearts in noble-minded holiness," he prayed for the Thessalonians. "What God asks of you is that you sanctify yourselves." And again: "The life to which God has called you . . . is a life of holiness."

To the Hebrews: "Brethren and saints, you share a heavenly calling." God comes to us to "give us a share in that holiness which is His."

The Holy Spirit guided Peter to be no less emphatic. "You must be holy in all the ordering of your lives."

"Your mortal life must be ordered by God's will, not by human appetites."

And how beautifully Peter described spiritual progress: "And you too have to contribute every effort on your part, crowning your faith with virtue, and virtue with enlightenment, and enlightenment with continence, and continence with endurance, and endurance with holiness, and holiness with brotherly love, and brotherly love with charity."

But it is our Lord who says it best: "Be perfect, as your heavenly Father is perfect."

Does this not mean that sanctity for the sincere Christian should be as normal as "growing up"? We plant a seed and it becomes a bush; this is nature's law of growth. A child is conceived and born and becomes an adult; again, the law of growth. In Baptism we are endowed with supernatural life and an almost limitless capacity for spiritual growth.

What adulthood is on the physical level, sainthood is meant to be on the spiritual level. Sanctity should be normal. To be a spiritual baby all our lives, a petrified dwarf, this is abnormal.

Why then is it that we do not grow to the holiness to which God has called us? Is it because we do not apply to our spiritual life the kind of exercise it requires? How does an athlete develop his physical powers? By pushing himself to the limit of his abilities, and by this means constantly developing a little more strength, a little more spring, a little more speed.

How does a student extend the capacity of his mind? By progressively harder mental exercise.

When someone asked Thomas Aquinas how to become a saint, he answered in two words: "Will it."

And when someone asked Francis de Sales how to learn to love God, he replied in three words: "By loving Him." When his questioner persisted, Francis said in effect: that is the only answer and the only way. We learn to love God by loving Him, and each act of love causes us to love Him more.

Just as the athlete learns to run a four-minute mile by running again and again to the limit of his present ability, and consequently stretching his capacity, so we can grow to love God like the saints by willing to love Him to the limit of our present ability. Few can ever be capable of the four-minute mile, but everyone, through God's abundant grace, is capable of sanctity.

When we act in accordance with the full degree of love that is presently ours, God gives us more love and we grow in love, which is to say in holiness. When we act with less love of God than is ours, we prepare the way not for growth in love but for its decrease.

But what is loving God? Is it not simply doing what He wants, and even more being what He wants, because He wants it? Because *He* wants it, that is the key. Most of the good deeds we do because we want them, because we expect praise, reward, or at least a sense of interior satisfaction. The difference between the saints and us is that God's will for the present moment was their rule of life. Whether they worked or played or prayed, they were not so much working or playing or praying as they were doing what they believed God wanted them to be doing at that moment.

They did what we do; but they did it for God. And we, too, must learn and practice doing just what we normally do, only not because it is our will but because it is His.

Chapter Eight

The Saints Were
Like Us

The Lord's treatment of His heroes of holiness does seem odd at times.

Joseph of Cupertino flew through the air with the greatest of ease. Did he want to?

Evil spirits physically attacked John Vianney, the renowned Cure d'Ars.

Catherine of Siena lived for years with her only food being the Blessed Host.

Like "man bites dog," this, in the literature of the saints, is news, and spiritual writers have made the most of it. But they did us, and we do ourselves, a disservice in dwelling too long and admiringly on these external byproducts of sanctity.

The saints themselves, realizing that the grace to conceal a grace is no small blessing, applied to these incidents our Lord's own words, "Tell no man of this."

Teresa of Avila was sometimes observed in mystical rapture and on occasion suspended bodily above the ground. Definitely she did not want this. She forthrightly describes her distaste, "I would very often resist, and exert all my strength, particularly when the rapture was coming on me in public. I did so, too, very often when I was alone, because I was afraid of delusions."

Once she says she felt a rapture and levitation coming on "when we were all together in choir, and I, on my knees, on the point of communicating. It was a very sore distress to me; for I thought it a most extraordinary thing, and was afraid it would occasion much talk; so I commanded the nuns—for it happened after I was Prioress—never to speak of it."

One can sense in her words a kind of chagrin that the good Lord should so embarrass her—as though she felt, while submissive to His will, that this was, if not beneath the dignity of His majesty, surely no way to treat a lady. She goes on to say that the moment she felt "that Our Lord was about to repeat the feat, and once, in particular, during a sermon—it was the feast of our house, some great ladies being present—I threw myself on the ground; then the nuns came around to hold me; but still the rapture was observed.

"I made many supplications to Our Lord," she confesses, "that He would be pleased to give me no more of these graces which were outwardly visible."

This Spanish mystic, a woman of profoundly practical judgment, came to feel deeply that to dwell on the preternatural was to emphasize the superficial at the cost of the essential.

We are prone to think of holiness in superficial, unrealistic terms. In particular we think of sanctity as doing something rather than as being someone. We tend to stress what the saints accomplished rather than what they were, which is a little like being content with looking at an orange rather than eating it.

We think in terms of canonization. The result is that we say to ourselves: So few are canonized; how can I be a saint? Or in terms of the saints, they founded orders, ransomed captives, established dozens of schools or hospitals. All these are quite outside our realm of reasonable expectations. Or, we think of nights the saints spent in contemplation, practiced violent mortifications, had mystical experiences. If these are required for holiness, how can we be holy?

But does this not attribute to God a niggardliness that, but for our ignorance, would be a most terrible insult? Surely the God of love could not love any of us so little as to deny us the opportunity to become heroic in holiness. Surely He wishes each of us to give back to Him the gift of love He first bestowed on us.

Most of us who are parents have had the sweet experience of having our small sons or daughters ask for a dime or quarter a few days before Christmas. We know why the request was made—the child wants to buy Mommy or Daddy a gift. And when the bar of candy, package of gum, pair of shoelaces, or whatever is presented to us at Christmas, we are as delighted by this token of love as by anything we receive, however costly. Can it be that God asks more of us than we ask of our little ones? Can it be that He loves us less, understands us less?

Surely all that God asks is that we take the coin of His gifts and turn them into a token of love to give back to Him. And His scales, insensitive to size, measure only love.

Our misconceptions of the nature of holiness are responsible in no small degree for the prevalence of spiritual mediocrity. This is why so many of us accept almost as axiomatic the fallacy that normal persons should not aspire to sanctity; that to do so smacks of presumption, even borders on the immodest, like a political hack aspiring to the presidency of the United States.

Our attitude toward the saints is not too unlike the attitude of my generation, as boys, toward the Four Horsemen of Notre Dame. In our hero worship we conceived of them as supermen, so superior to the players on our local college team that any comparison was, athletically speaking, sacrilegious. It took a long time for me, at least, to outgrow this childish fantasy. In fact, I had to see some of the members of that fabled backfield close up and in civilian clothes before I could settle for the truth that they were just a little better—and a little better coached—than other good football players of their era.

We fail to realize that the saints were like us and that what they became is not unattainable for us. Instead, we tend to think of them as actors and actresses in a kind of play; as though they knew all the time what their future held; and so they could prepare to carry out their clearly defined roles. Act One—a special call from God. Act Two—mystical prayer, levitations, miracles, wholesale conversions. Act Three—the seventh mansion, spiritual marriage, and transforming union.

Actually the saints, generally speaking, were quite as much in the dark about their futures as we are about ours.

In other ways, too, they were like us. Too often we forget that Peter was a fisherman, Luke a doctor, Paul a tentmaker who paid his own way as a missionary. Camillus was a soldier, as were Ignatius, Sabastian, Joan, and others. Ives was a lawyer, as was Thomas More. Wilfred was a baker, Julian an innkeeper, Andronicus a barber, Isadore a farmer, Gerard a tailor. Margaret of Cortona was a seamstress, Notburga a kitchen maid.

Camillus liked to gamble, but was probably not too good at it. Ignatius enjoyed dancing and billiards and was probably skilled at both. John Bosco was an acrobat and an amateur magician.

Among the saints were kings and queens, servants and beggars, geniuses and dullards, teachers and students, octogenarians and children, virgins and mothers of families, large and small.

Some lived lives distinguished by holiness almost from birth. But others were notorious sinners for much of their lives. No fault that any of us has was unknown to some of them. Camillus's terrible temper was so bad that, added to his gambling, it kept him constantly in trouble for years. Margaret of Cortona was seduced by a nobleman and lived with him out of wedlock for nine years. Catherine of Genoa, married to an unfaithful husband, gave herself over for a time to somewhat riotous living. Among the saints are some who are capable of saying to the worst of our generation, "Anything you can do, I could do better"—or "worse" is a more accurate term.

They were like us. We can be like them in the one thing that matters—love.

Chapter Nine

Holiness Lies in
What We Are

It is in the inner life that holiness resides. For centuries during the Middle Ages, the emphasis was on terrible physical austerity: severe fasting, bloody scourgings, hair shirts. The reaction against seeking holiness through extreme bodily chastisement owes much to such saints as Francis de Sales. In proposing a rule for the visitation order he sought "less rigor for the body—more gentleness of heart." He thought it unwise for the nuns to be "more intent on keeping their stomachs free from meat than their minds free from self-will."

The correct order, for Francis, was first to form the inner man, and after this to "set the outer life right." In his *Introduction to the Devout Life,* he wrote, "I could never agree with the method of those who begin the formation of man with the outer posture of the body, the clothes and the hair. I believe that one must begin within."

In one of his spiritual conferences, he told a little story on himself. "When I was a young student," he said, "I was seized with a fervor and a great longing to be saintly and perfect. I began by fancying that, in order to become so, I must twist my head on one side when I was saying my breviary, because another student who really was a saint did so." Then followed the wry observation: "This practice I continued steadily for some time, but without becoming any holier."

While in our day the outer posture is no longer so heavily stressed, we do seem to be in some danger of substituting something only a little less superficial. We are too preoccupied with doing, rather than with being.

"We flatter ourselves that we are doing what God desires of us," writes Father Leen in *In the Likeness of Christ.* "If only we fling ourselves with earnestness and zeal into the accomplishment of the duties that the state of life we have embraced imposes on us."

But then we become so caught up in the work that we make our goal the perfection of the work rather than the perfection of ourselves. What may have truly begun as a work for God ends as something done out of ambition, vainglory, or the desire for praise. We begin by seeking God in our work. We end by seeking ourselves.

Somehow we find it terribly difficult to build our lives on the principle that God is not nearly so interested in what we do for Him as in what we are for Him. The pressures of modern society stress doing, getting ahead, making a name. These are the measuring rods of worldly success, and they have infiltrated the spiritual outlook.

But as Augustine said, "God seeks thee more than thy gifts." And this is wholly logical, first, because the person is superior to the gift, and, second, because what we give ultimately depends on who we are.

We might think that what God wanted of Thérèse was her *Autobiography,* which has influenced so many millions for good. But no, what He wanted of Thérèse was that she be the "Little Flower," allowing Him to make of her whatever He wished. Her story is wonderful because she was wonderful.

Saul, the Pharisee, had to become Paul, the Christ-lover, before the Lord let him do anything at all. He took him aside and made him the person He wanted him to be: first, by striking him down on the road to Damascus; then, by sending Ananias to him; next by leading him into the desert for years of preparation; then by permitting him a fortnight in Jerusalem; finally, by more years of preparation at home in Tarsus.

Only when God had led Paul across the bridge from Judaism to Christianity, made him reborn, a new creation, did He permit him to evangelize and preach and write. What Paul did grew out of who Paul was—and who Paul was was far greater than what Paul did.

God did not write a set of specifications for His greatest missionary such as man would have written. Man would have made him incomparably eloquent. But Paul refers to himself as "unexperienced in speaking," "without any high pretensions to eloquence," as preaching "not with an orator's cleverness," "full of anxious fear," and "so diffident when he meets you face to face." Paul knew how it felt to put an audience to sleep.

In the Acts we read that Paul preached in Troas one evening until midnight, and a young man named Eutychus sitting in an open window fell asleep and tumbled from the third story to the ground. He was killed. Paul went down, bent over him, embraced him, and restored him to life—then went back upstairs, commemorated the Last Supper, and went on speaking until dawn.

Had he been able to preach "with an orator's cleverness," Paul says, the result perhaps would have been that "the cross of Christ might be robbed of its force." Instead God used "a foolish thing, our preaching, to save those who will believe. . . . So much wiser than men is God's foolishness; so much stronger than men is God's weakness" (1 Cor 1:17–25).

Action will come. One cannot love God deeply without expressing it in deeds. But our action must flow from the love that is in us. Otherwise we are in danger of substituting God's tasks for God. Let us be the someone God has destined—then there will be no question but that we will do what He has planned for us.

Chapter Ten

What Must We Do, Lord?

Near the city of Damascus one sunny day around noon, sometime after our Lord's death, one of the most awesome sentences ever recorded was spoken—"SAUL, SAUL, WHY DO YOU PERSECUTE ME?" With these words the Roman Jew who was to become the greatest of all missionaries was introduced to the risen Christ and to the fundamental concept that permeates his writings, that of the Mystical Body.

It must have been as one breathing fire against the Christians that Saul approached the ancient city. With what tireless energy had he been delivering Christians into chains and prisons and testifying against them to their deaths! What was he thinking as he approached Damascus, his new hunting ground? Was he reviewing in his mind elaborate plans for entrapping the enemy when the noonday brightness of the sun was eclipsed by an even more brilliant light that shone from heaven and enveloped him in such blinding rays that he fell to the ground and lay there trembling, pinned by a force he had no power to resist?

It was then that he heard the terrifying question: "Saul—Saul—why . . . ?"

"Who are you?" he asked, though he may have suspected, for he added, "Lord." "Who are you, Lord?"

"I am Jesus whom you persecute."

And Saul, whose whole life had been bound up in the observance of the Jewish Law—Saul, who could not accept the Resurrection because to do so would set Jesus of Nazareth above the Law—Saul now suddenly had to accept the Resurrection because here and now he saw the glorified body of Jesus—Saul surrendered unconditionally with the words, "Lord, what shall I do?"

What must Saul do? He must "rise up and go into the city" where he would be told. Thenceforth, for the next several years, before beginning his missionary journeys to convert the world, he must learn what it means to be fully a Christian.

So it is with us. To respond to the invitation that we be heroic in holiness, "perfect as your heavenly Father is perfect," we need to ask again and again, "What must I do, Lord?" And the answer in essence will always be the same: Learn what it means to be fully a Christian. Learn to see Christ in others. But, above all, "put on Christ" until, as with Paul, He takes possession of us so that we think with His mind, will with His will, and act with, in, and through Him.

How? Through the means Christ Himself provided to make us full participants in His Mystical Body.

It would be unbelievable, had our Lord not said it, that He, with His Church, forms one body, which in the phrase of Augustine is the whole Christ. Our Lord's word makes it not only believable but certain; yet it remains a mystery, the meaning of which can be approached only through similitudes.

Our Lord Himself used the analogy of a vine or tree. As the branch of a tree contains the life of the tree within itself, so we contain His life in us.

Paul used the analogy of the body. Our own body has many parts, yet is one. The head, mouth, eyes, nose, ears, arms, legs, hands, and feet all have different functions, yet comprise one body, animated by one spirit. So, too, Christ's Mystical Body comprises many members and yet is one.

Others have used still other illustrations. As many grains of wheat combine to make one loaf of bread, and many drops of water combine to make the sea, so also many individuals are incorporated into one Mystical Body and this Body is Christ Himself.

For this reason our Lord could say, "Saul, Saul, why do you persecute *Me*?"

And for this reason Paul could write, "All you who have been baptized in Christ's name have put on the person of Christ . . . you are all one person in Jesus Christ" (Gal 3:27–28).

For this reason, we can declare with the certainty of faith that, being a member of Christ, we are one with Him. We dwell in Him and He in us. We dwell in the Father and He in us. We dwell in the Holy Spirit and He also in us. We dwell in the Trinity, and the Trinity dwells in us.

Christ is Christ, and we are we—separate and distinct—yet we are one with Him.

So, when we ask, "What must we do, Lord?" The answer comes: Realize, as best you can, your dignity as a Christian.

We must strive to realize that as surely as our hand or foot is united to our own body, even more surely are we united with Christ.

We must realize—a shattering thought!—that closely as Christ's own Mother was joined to Him *naturally,* we are even more closely joined to Him *supernaturally.* Surely, this is what He meant when He answered the one who told him that His Mother and brothers were waiting outside, by pointing to His disciples and saying: "He who does the will of my Father in heaven is my brother, my sister, my mother" (Mt 12:50).

But always the question persists: How? How can this be? We cannot say. All we know is that at the moment when our Lord offered Himself to His Father in His Passion and death, mankind's mystical union with Him came into being—and our own personal union with Him came into existence potentially. Our union became actual the moment we received faith in Baptism. In that flashing instant, the Father accepted us as His adopted child, a coheir with Christ.

So much did we become one with Him that His crucifixion became our crucifixion; His death on the cross, our death; His right to heaven, our right to heaven. We are sharers in His atonement, just as if we had died in atonement ourselves.

And if again we ask how this can be, the answer is that it not only *can* be—it *is*—because the grace that was given to Christ was given Him not only as an individual but as the head of His Church, so that grace flows from Him into all His members. Our Lord's actions, as Thomas Aquinas explains, have the same relation to Himself and to His members as the actions of a man in the state of grace have to the man himself. Whatever our Lord did, therefore, is ours as though we had done it ourselves.

And just as Christ on Calvary was mankind—you and I—making atonement, so in the Mass, He is mankind—you and I—making atonement and giving glory, praise, and thanksgiving to the Trinity. This is the utterly incomprehensible dignity of a Christian.

But "what must we do, Lord?" We must realize that from this dignity flows an equally incomprehensible responsibility. Since there is this oneness between Christ and all His members, whatever we do to the least of our brothers, we do to Him. Smile on a neighbor and we smile on Christ. Give blood to the ailing and we give it to Him. Feed a baby or hold it lovingly and we repeat and renew the actions of Mary holding and feeding her babe. Thus Christ enables us to repay Him a little for what He has done for us. Thus He makes our love and our service both His and ours.

Chapter Eleven

A Place of Our Own

It is vital that we realize this presence of Christ in "the least of these." For it is our loving intention that measures the worth of all that we do.

What if we frown rather than smile, reject rather than give, hate rather than love? Then, just as it hurts the whole human body when a part of it is injured, so hurt is done to the Mystical Body when one of its members denies Christ by acting in an un-Christlike manner.

Just as every act of conformity to God's will is an act of union with Christ, so every act of rebellion is a denial of union with Christ, an act of disunion. Every sin is an attack upon the whole Mystical Body.

Then, our hope is in Christ's prayer, "Father, forgive them; they know not what they do."

But again we ask, "What must we do, Lord?" To be fully a Christian we must realize that we are, each of us, unique. Our corporate existence in the Mystical Body does not nullify our individuality. Just as the hand is part of the body and yet has a function uniquely its own that no other part of the body is fully capable of duplicating, so each of us, while united to the Body, has a uniqueness in God's eyes.

What a wonderful thought it is that God has marked out for each of us a place of our own!

In all the world that has existed from the time of Adam to the present, there never has been—among all the billions of persons who now inhabit the earth, there is not—and in all the ages to come no matter how long the world shall last, there can never be another you, or another me.

Each you among the readers of this page came into existence through a unique act of God's creative love. Each you continues to live because at every instant He renews this unique act of creative love. You *are* because He wanted you to *be,* an individual you, a unique you, the only you that can ever be.

In each you, He sees something individual, something desirable that does not exist in precisely the same way in any other person, not even His own Mother.

On the north wall of the National Shrine of the Immaculate Conception in Washington, DC, there looks down on worshipers and visitors alike a huge and compellingly beautiful mosaic of Christ. Each piece in that mosaic is different; ordered to contribute a certain color, shape, or background to the whole design. This piece reacts to the light so as to reflect redness; this one, blueness; this, yellow; this, purple; this brown.

So, with each of us. We are to react to the light of God's grace so as to reflect Christ, to reflect Him not only to the world but to the sight of God Himself.

We are, each of us, a piece of the Father's mosaic of the Christ.

There is one sense in which each piece of a mosaic is capable of being the most important. If just one piece of the mosaic of Christ in the Shrine of the Immaculate Conception were missing, is it too much to believe that its absence would have a greater impact on the attention of the designer than all the other pieces? So it is with us in the divine plan, we who are all bits of the mosaic of Christ on earth. When one of us fails to reflect his or her portion of the image of Christ, the gap is so noticeable that God the designer, our Lord the Good Shepherd, must leave the ninety-nine or the nine-thousand-nine-hundred-ninety-nine pieces that are in place and go seeking for that which is lost.

The parable of the Good Shepherd is a wonderful illustration of our uniqueness in God's sight.

So, to be fully Christian, we must understand that each of us in the Mystical Body has a place of his own and for each of us God has a plan of His own. It is literally true that God has planned our entire life. Our happiness not only hereafter, but here and now, consists in finding and heroically following that plan.

So, once more the question: "Lord, what must we do?" To be fully Christian we must strive to be the saint God wants us to be, not the saint *we* want to be.

In responding to God's invitation to be heroes of holiness, the saints desired to be precisely what God intended for them. We who are not saints are intent on being what we ourselves intend. We tell ourselves: I will serve God gloriously by being a great influence, a magnetic reformer, a magnificent missionary, converting whole nations like St. Francis Xavier. I will be a masterful speaker, golden-voiced like St. John Chrysostom. I will found a society or an institute like St. Ignatius. I will write a profound book on mystical prayer like St. Teresa. It would be nice to be a saint if we could be as one of these.

It is as though the piece of glass designed to give redness said, "I want to reflect blueness." Or as if the round fragment said, "I want to be hexagonal." Or the piece in the corner said, "I want to be in the center."

No one can be heroic in holiness on his or her own terms. We can be holy at all only on God's terms. Only if we are content to follow His design for us in complete abandonment; desiring nothing that is not part of His plan, refusing nothing that is; content to live at this moment of time, in this land and community, following the particular career that is ours; satisfied with the emotional, mental, and physical equipment He has bestowed; accepting whatever consolations or desolations may be ours; full of humble wonderment that our God is at all interested, much less so intimately interested in us; grateful in short to be our unique selves in the Mystical Body—only then are we truly heroic, and only then are we fully Christian.

No saint has ever been a saint *in general*. Each has been *uniquely* God's saint—or has not been one at all. This is the long and short of it. This is what we must be.

Modern man lives in a fool's paradise. He doesn't know his own place in the world. It is natural for man to act as though he is the center of the universe. But, of course, he isn't. And until man comes to understand that he is not the center of the universe, he cannot keep his place at all.

One of the problems of our day is that we fail to see God's plan for us, God's plan for the world, and our place in it. It's as though we were in a forest and we concentrated completely on looking at just one tree. Concentrating solely on this one tree, we could not understand, we could not realize where we were.

We must stand off from ourselves from time to time and think about this fact that we are *not* the center of the universe. It is not easy to do this. Our consciousness is such that it causes us to look at everything as revolving around us, as happening to us. Intellectually, we know that is not true—but we have to think about it, to meditate on it—otherwise we forget this truth. It is impossible for us to truly realize that we are only one person out of *billions* now living in the world—yet we must try to see ourselves in this context from time to time. How often do we take time to try to give a conception of what it really means to be just *one* of *billions* of people?

Not long ago, I flew in a plane across the Atlantic. Up in that plane, it was utterly impossible for me to realize how different it would be if I were down on the Atlantic in a rowboat. Here we were flying across the ocean at a speed of 560 miles per hour, 35,000 feet above sea level. There was an interval during the flight when the plane began to bounce around sharply. My neighbor, who happened to be an official of the airline, told me that there were severe storms over the Atlantic and though we were nearly seven miles high, we were feeling the effects of what was going on below us.

I tried to imagine what it must be like on the ocean itself, in a small boat, with the wind raging and the waves rising to heights of fifty or seventy-five feet—nature in one of her wild moods. How helpless anyone would be. But I could have no accurate conception of what it must have been like. The violence of the sea was a fact down there—but up where we were, we had almost no conception at all of what was really going on.

This is how it is with us throughout our lives. We have very little realization of what is going on all around us. In this sense, we have lost touch with reality. God, of course, is the ultimate reality. Yet, we have a tendency to exclude God from our lives—as though He didn't exist. We act as though—if there is a God—He is much too busy to be interested in us anyway.

But if God is not interested, why do we have the Eucharist? Isn't the Eucharist proof par excellence that God is *tremendously* interested in and concerned about us—that He is totally, extravagantly, intimately interested, in you and me? Why otherwise should He come to us individually as our faith tells us He does? Why would He go to such pains to make Himself available to us?

If we are going to get a clear conception of what life is all about, we have to think about it from time to time in terms of our place in the totality of existence—in terms of God's plan for us and for the world as revealed by Christ.

Not that we should, or could, think about this constantly, all the time. We'd never get anything else done. Our consciousness is such—and so planned by God—that we do see the world as revolving around us, everything happening to us. But in the back of our minds we should have the realization that though it seems this way, it is not really so. We have to get a balance between the consciousness that everything revolves around us and the actual truth that our intellect reveals that we are not the center—that we are just a fragment of reality—that we are really infinitesimal in relation to the whole. We have to see ourselves in terms of God's plan for man as a whole—not just us—but our part in the entirety.

The early Fathers of the Church preached this view. If we read St. Paul, we see that again and again he talked about and wrote about the totality of God's plan. He tells how it was in the fullness of time that Christ came, that this was ordained from the beginning. The other preachers and writers also had a keen vision of salvation on history—the whole history of God's plan—the totality of His plan.

We need to do more of this. Otherwise, we shall continue to live in the fool's paradise of believing that we are the center of the universe and consequently living for ourselves.

Chapter Twelve

Let Us Be What We Are

No other group of men or women has been so great as the saints. None has been so noble of character, so valiant and self-sacrificing. None has contributed so effectively to the happiness and progress of mankind. The greatest heroes and heroines the world has known, or knows today, are the heroic in holiness.

Yet how seldom do we advert to this truth.

One can travel through the countries of Europe and the historic heroes we meet are Napoleon and Churchill, Beethoven and Mozart, Shakespeare and Goethe, Michelangelo and Rembrandt. All these, surely, were great in accomplishment. But they were not as truly heroic as were Vincent de Paul, Francis of Assisi, Teresa of Avila, Ignatius Loyola, and Thomas More.

Even if accomplishment be the measuring rod, the "armies" of Ignatius have ranged farther and conquered more than

Napoleon's ever did—and brought learning and peace with them rather than destruction and death.

The legacy bequeathed to posterity by Vincent, Francis, and Teresa undoubtedly contains seeds of happiness and growth unequalled by that, great as it is, left by Shakespeare and Michelangelo.

As for qualities of soul—courage, perseverance, self-sacrifice, humility, love—there can be no question where superiority lies.

They stand larger than life in the corridors of history. It is in holiness that the truest heroism is to be found.

This most genuine of heroism is within the reach of all. Granted, all are not destined to be equally holy. But surely it is true that we are invited and called and urged to a perfection so far above what we are presently achieving that if we do achieve it we most certainly will be true saints.

If sanctity consists in *being* some*one* rather than in *doing* some*thing*—and if the some*one* each of us is called to be as a member of the Mystical Body is unique—then it follows that sanctity consists in being that some*one* in the most complete and best way possible.

"Let us be completely what we are," said Francis de Sales. When he and others of like mind put forth this concept three-and-a-half centuries ago, it was a revolutionary idea for their generation. Despite our emphasis—almost our obsession—concerning self-fulfillment, it is still quite revolutionary today.

This is rather odd, surely, because the uniqueness of the individual member of the Mystical Body, and the consequent necessity of being completely what one is, was a keynote of early Christian spirituality. Paul, especially, drummed it into those he was instructing.

"Everyone has his own vocation to which he has been called," he wrote to the Corinthians. "Let him keep to it" (1 Cor 7:20).

There are "different kinds of gifts," and "different kinds of service," and "different manifestations of power" (1 Cor 12:4–6).

"God has given us different positions in the Church, apostles first, then prophets, and thirdly teachers; then come miraculous powers, then gifts of healing, works of mercy, the management of affairs, speaking with different tongues, and interpreting prophecy" (1 Cor 12:28–29).

"If a man is a prophet, let him prophesy as far as the measure of his faith will let him. The administrator must be content with his administration, the teacher with his work of teaching, the preacher with his preaching. Each must perform his own task well . . ." (Rom 12:6–8).

Surely, this expresses essentially the same thought as "let us be completely what we are." But somehow the notion survives that being completely what we are is not enough. Sanctity is so abnormal, it is thought, and its attainment so extraordinarily difficult that it is virtually impossible to achieve while living in this world. Thus by the fourth century some writers and preachers were urging everyone, if he or she would be holy, to practice continence and strict asceticism and to withdraw from the world.

Even before this, a similar error had been made by some who saw in the supreme sacrifice of martyrdom the sure road to sanctity. While desire to be a martyr seems, and often is, noble, it can be a delusion. The early Church encouraged no one to seek martyrdom. Peter and Paul and the other apostles took all reasonable means to preserve their lives. Others, overly ambitious and even presumptuous, deliberately put themselves in the way of persecution; and, under the torments inflicted, some denied Christ.

Through the centuries there have been those who, trusting unduly in their own powers, have vowed virginity and retired to monasteries or the desert; then finding themselves unfitted by nature to the austere life, many have not only missed their goal but eventually left the faith. Of how many priests and nuns this has been true in our own day, who shall say?

The error is not in desiring and striving to be holy. It is in seeking to be someone other than God intends; seeking holiness not in being completely what we are, but in forming ourselves according to our own mistaken notions.

Chapter Thirteen

Love Is the Common Denominator

There is no question but that, objectively, the religious state is higher than the lay state; nor that holy virginity is higher than marriage. But it does not follow that one who is capable of achieving a certain perfection in marriage is capable of achieving a higher perfection in virginity. On the contrary, it is possible for the individual to be much less than perfect in the more perfect state when he could be far more nearly perfect in the less perfect state.

The obvious fact is that most of us are called by God to marriage and life in the world. For us to disregard nature and seek another state of life because it is objectively more perfect is not to serve God but either to misread our own capabilities or to succumb to foolish ambition. It is not unlike the mother of James and John asking: "Here are my two sons; grant that in thy kingdom one may take his place on thy right and the other on thy left" (Mt 20:21).

It is as possible to reach highest perfection in the world as in the desert or the cloister. "Perfection does not consist in not seeing the world, but in not giving oneself over to it inwardly." This sentiment was strongly reinforced by Pope Pius XI who said in his encyclical on the saint: "Francis de Sales appears given to the Church through God's special decree so as to counter that point of view deeply rooted in his time and not overcome today which says that true saintliness . . . is so difficult to achieve that the majority of the faithful could not possibly attain it."

We serve God best when we give back to Him as completely as possible what He has first given us; in other words, when we follow the sanctity that corresponds to our unique nature and circumstances of life. This is the milieu in which we are each to seek perfection.

What makes heroic holiness possible for all is love. This is so beautifully described by Thérèse of Lisieux in her *Autobiography* when she tells of her delight in finding her "vocation," the "niche God has appointed for me." She had been tormented by unfulfilled longings, as if she could never satisfy the needs of her nature without performing for our Lord's sake "every kind of heroic action at once." She found her answer in Paul's famous passage on charity.

"Charity is the best way of all because it leads straight to God," Thérèse comments. "Now I was at peace; when St. Paul was talking about the different members of the Mystical Body I couldn't recognize myself in any of them; or rather I could recognize myself in all of them. But charity—that was the key to my vocation . . . Love, in fact, is the vocation which includes all others; it's a universe of its own, comprising all time and space—it's eternal."[1] There are, in other words, as many forms of sanctity as there are saints. The common denominator of all is love—love of God and of God's will. If charity is lacking, *all* is lacking. If charity is present, *all* is present.

But what precisely does it mean to be completely what we are? It means, first, to accept with the fullest consent of our will our present state in life, our personality, physical and mental equipment, our general health, our assets and liabilities, and all our circumstances. These are what we have from God. These are what we have to give back to Him.

We must recognize that God does not wish us to be famous, rich, talented, or popular at this time—unless we are. He does not wish us to be married at this time—unless we are. He does not wish us to be a martyr, or to give all our wealth to the poor, or to spend nights in contemplative prayer—unless these conform to our state and circumstances in life.

If we are parents, He does not want us to become so engrossed in social work, or church work, or even in our professions or businesses that we flee from our family circle night after night to the neglect and unhappiness of spouse and children. He desires husbands and wives, first and foremost, to love each other and be the best husbands and wives they can. He desires mothers and fathers to guide their children with love and patience and be the best mothers and fathers they can.

This does not mean a shirking of responsibilities that come to us in virtue of our divided responsibilities. Though the primary responsibility of married persons is to each other and their family, this does not nullify reasonable responsibilities that we may have as employers or employees, as members of the parish, as citizens of a community, state, and nation. All these responsibilities must be dovetailed according to our reasonable judgments.

Being completely what we are means also seeking the virtues that are proper to our state and circumstances of life. Thus the home must not be made a monastery or a convent, for this is to introduce a way of life that is unsuitable. Devotions and pious practices that actually interfere with our calling are to be avoided.

Francis de Sales bluntly contradicted a spiritual director who advised a woman that it was "better if she prayed instead of looking after her household affairs, even if it made her husband unhappy." Francis said that spirituality is exercised in different ways, "each according to his character and vocation," and it must also be adapted to "the strength, the employment, and the duties of each one in particular."

Is it fit, we are asked, "that a bishop should lead the solitary life of a Carthusian? Or that married people should lay up no greater store of goods than the Capuchin? If a tradesman were to remain the whole day in church, like a member of a religious order . . . would not such devotion be ridiculous, unorganized and insupportable? . . . Devotion . . . when it goes contrary to our lawful vocation, then without doubt it is false."[2]

The religious has his rule of life. The husband, the wife, the mother, the father, the unmarried, each has his or her rule also: the duties of his state and circumstances in life.

Finally, being completely what we are means living what we are to the full; really trying to be the best husband and father, wife and mother we can; really trying to be the best employer or employee we can; really trying to be the best neighbor or parishioner or citizen we can. Isn't it true that we live most of our lives at about half capacity so that we're like a car chugging up a hill with half its cylinders misfiring? Are we really trying to be the unique someone God made us to be?

"Let us be completely what we are." And we who are married, let us get rid forever of the puritanical notion that for two persons to be passionately in love is somehow to rule out their being even more completely in love with God. A powerful antidote to this poisonous concept is the life of St. Elizabeth of Hungary. Of all the heroines of literature, of all the lovers of history, none loved more passionately than Elizabeth her husband; and she was a great saint. When her husband went off to the Crusade, Elizabeth went with him to the edge of the kingdom and had to be carried away almost by force. They loved so much it was almost painful to be out of each other's sight.

But when Elizabeth's husband died on the Crusade and, much later, she knelt beside his coffin she offered a prayer that is a model of devotion and conformity to the will of God:

> You know, O Lord . . . that I loved him more than anything in this world, because he loved You and because he was my husband. Thou knowest that all my life I should have been glad to live with him in want and wretchedness,

to beg my bread from door to door, only to have the happiness of being with him. But as it has pleased You to take him to Yourself, I am perfectly resigned to Your Holy Will. And if by saying one Our Father, I could recall him to life against Your Will, I would not say it. Only this I ask: grant unto him eternal rest and to me grace to serve You faithfully until my last breath.

Behold the prayer of one who was *completely* what she was.

Notes

1. *Autobiography of St. Thérèsè of Lisieux,* trans. by Ronald Knox, (New York: P.J. Kennedy & Sons, 1962), 235.

2. Francis de Sales, *Introduction to the Devout Life*, trans. John K. Ryan, (New York: Harper, 1966), 6.

Chapter Fourteen

God Speaks to Us in the Present Moment

The ideal of being completely what we are in the best possible way seems obvious, simple, and perfectly natural. But how is it applied in practice? Undoubtedly, holiness consists in faithfully following God's plan for us as unique persons, each of us being the person He wishes. But how do we know His plan for us? How do we know the precise person He desires us to be?

We don't know, of course, the precise person God wants us to be ten, five, or even two years from now. We don't know His precise plan for us even two minutes from now.

We are like the little boy whom the pastor asked, "Who made you?"

"God."

"What did God make you to be?"

"I dunno. I ain't done yet."

We know God's general plan: holiness, sanctity, putting on Christ. We know that we are to carry out this plan by fidelity to His commandments and the precepts of the Church, and by fulfilling the duties of our particular state and circumstances of life.

But is this all we have to go on? Certainly not. While we cannot know God's precise plan for us two minutes hence, we can know, down to the minutest detail, His plan for us at *this* moment. We can know exactly the kind of person He wants us to be here and now.

We can know this because God speaks to us at every instant—through all that He permits to happen to us, to touch us, at this and every moment. Nothing occurs without His knowledge and permission. The whole of holiness consists in recognizing God in every circumstance of the present moment and conforming our will to His will as this moment reveals it. At every occurrence writes Jean-Pierre de Caussade, "we should say: Dominus est. It is the Lord."

Surely this is the essence of the life of every saint who ever lived.

The classic development of this doctrine, that each moment is the manifestation of the will of God, is that of the Jesuit Caussade, who lived more than two centuries ago. "Things indeed proceed like words out of the mouth of God," he wrote in *Self-Abandonment to Divine Providence.* "God creates at each moment a divine thought which is signified by a created thing . . . What happens at each moment bears the imprint of the will of God and of His adorable name."

Holiness, therefore, "corresponds to the love we have for God's good pleasure," by which Caussade means God's designs, will, or action of the present moment. The more His will and designs are loved, no matter what they may ordain, the greater is the sanctity."

Here, then, is the difference between ordinary holiness and heroic holiness. The faithful observance of the commandments and the fulfillment of the duties of our state of life make us holy. But adding to this the loving acceptance of God's designs as they are revealed moment by moment, and the loving submission to the crosses that are constantly being presented to us—this can make us heroically holy.

And this is why the highest perfection is possible for the lay person as well as for the monk or the nun, for the laborer as for the chairman of the board, for the charwoman as for the president of the United States, for the illiterate peasant as for the pope.

It was the realization of this truth that led de Caussade to say with undisguised fervor, "O my God, how I should wish to be the missionary of Your holy will and teach everyone that there is nothing so easy, so ordinary and so ready to everyone's hand as holiness . . . Do what you are now doing, suffer what you are now suffering; to do all this with holiness, nothing need be changed but your hearts—sanctity therefore consists in willing what happens to us by God's design. Yes, holiness of heart is a simple *fiat*, a simple conformity of the will to God's will."

It is indeed so easily understood that we are likely to assume that it is equally easy to practice, just as we sometimes assume that St. Thérèse proposed nothing very difficult in her little way. Actually, the sweet exterior of the Little Flower concealed a will of iron, and it was thoroughly tested in her faithfulness to the practice of her little sacrifices. So, too, Father Caussade. On one occasion he was ordered by his superior to take on a task for which he had a great distaste and, as he thought, no aptitude. He confesses that he groaned, prayed, and offered to spend the rest of his life in the novitiate house at Toulouse if only he could be relieved of his assignment.

If it is a relief to us to find that others—even those of the stature of this good priest—discover a heavy cross in obedience. It is even more of an encouragement to learn that after Father Caussade, again and again, *willed* to make the sacrifice he embarked on his new assignment with "peace and liberty of spirit," and more than this remained "calm and in peace" in the midst of a multitude of problems and complications that normally would have overwhelmed him.

So while the practice is one that requires heroic perseverance, good will and prayer provide all that is necessary.

This carries over, of course, into our work. We do not have to be afraid to fail. When we have done what we honestly feel is our reasonable best, we can abandon the success of our efforts to Him. Unlike some worldly employers, God never insists on success—only on care and diligence in doing our part.

To quote Father Caussade again: "Often things go all right and I give thanks to God; sometimes everything goes wrong, I again bless His Holy Name and offer Him the sacrifice of my efforts. Once this sacrifice has been made, God arranges everything."

True, it does happen at times that we have more to do than we can accomplish in the period provided. Then all we can do is our best. And our best almost invariably is done when we work calmly and diligently rather than in feverish haste. While we are doing one thing, that is enough; we cannot do all our tasks at the same time. So we are to work calmly but not anxiously, steadily but not feverishly, taking each task as it comes, doing them one at a time. If, despite our best efforts, we do not finish or succeed and a reprimand follows, there should be no disquiet in what Francis de Sales calls the "higher" part of our soul, even though we may feel a natural disappointment.

This cross, too, is one that God permits us to bear; and if we bear it with loving acceptance, He *must* make of it not only what is good for us but what is best—so that this becomes the best that could happen to us as of that moment in God's total plan.

This is being completely what we are in the best possible way. This, says Francis de Sales in his *Spiritual Conferences*, "is the virtue of virtues; it is the cream of charity, the odor of humility, the merit, I consider, of patience, and the fruit of perseverance. Great is this virtue, and alone worthy of being practiced by the best beloved children of God."

This is not to say that "we shall never have desires contrary to the will of God or that nature will never shrink with repugnance from the dispositions of His good pleasure," Francis continues. But when this occurs, "we must remain at peace, and paying no attention whatever to what that lower nature desires, we must embrace the divine will and unite ourselves to it whatever this may entail."

In the last farewell that Francis spoke to the sisters of Lyons the evening before he died, the great bishop of Geneva left this message that is so clearly applicable to our day and our America:

> Do you ask what I desire should remain most deeply engraved upon your mind, so that you may put it to practice? Ah, my dear daughters, what shall I say, except these excellent words I have so often already recommended to you: Desire nothing, refuse nothing. These words say everything, for they teach us the practice of perfect indifference. Look upon the Infant Jesus in the Crib (this was the day after Christmas); He accepts poverty, nakedness, the company of brute beasts, all the inclemencies of the weather—all, in fact, that happens to Him by His Father's permission. We are never told that He stretched forth His little hands to His Mother's breast; He left her to provide all that was necessary to Him, but, at the same time, He never refused the little comforts which she gave Him. He received the services of St. Joseph, the adoration of the kings and of the shepherds, all with equal indifference. So, too, ought we to desire nothing and to refuse nothing, but to suffer and to receive with perfect evenness of mind all that the Providence of God may permit. May God give us grace to do this.

Chapter Fifteen

God Is in Charge

Not so long ago people were apparently much more interested in the providence of God than they are now. Books were written on the subject and chapters in many spiritual books emphasized this concept.

Today, however, man seems to have concluded that God's providence no longer has much place in his life. Man thinks, or assumes, that he himself is in charge. Rather than man being God's helper, God is now thought of as man's helper—if indeed man concludes that he needs any help at all other than that of science and technology.

This attitude has permeated into virtually all of man's activities: it is evident in a deteriorating prayer life, in lessened spiritual reading, in the action syndrome.

We can only be the losers by this. God is not less in charge today than He was two thousand or three thousand years ago, in the time of Jesus and the time of Moses. Sometimes God takes us at our own word, at our own evaluation of the situation. He can leave us to our own devices as so often He left the Jews, until they came back to Him pleading for help, recognizing their weakness, seeking his forgiveness.

Is this, perhaps, what the future holds for modern man?

God's providence *is* still supreme. He still rules all. He foresees, permits, and provides for all that occurs, even to the smallest event or detail.

God eternally beholds all things. All that has ever occurred, that is now taking place, or that will happen is seen by Him NOW. Like the author of a book or play who has clearly outlined all that his characters will do, be, or become, and who has the entire plot in mind, God sees the book of existence— all of it—sees it in eternity, sees it without change, sees it in a timeless now.

I remember once flying over a big city on a beautifully clear day that enabled me to see for many miles, to make out houses, churches, schools, cars, buses, a train, a crowd watching a football game. This panoramic view, which seemed to allow me to take in the life of a whole city at a glance and to see, in a way, what was going on simultaneously in various sections of the metropolis, made me think of God and His all-seeing vision of creation.

We might think of it like this. God sees all that He will ever create and sees each particle of it in its fullness, in all its phases and facets. He sees the effect on everything that exists of the laws He has created, the law of gravity, the laws of growth, the laws that cover gases; liquids, and solids, the laws of thermo dynamics, the special property of water that causes it to contract with lowering of temperature above freezing and then to expand on freezing. He sees the results of man's free will, how every person will use his or her free will in every free action of his or her life. He balances all these actions and reactions, all the events of history, those governed by natural law and those open to human freedom. He sees all that might be if He gave man less freedom or if He hedged man's freedom with different physical constraints. He judges man's intellect, the effects of human passion. He sees what use man will make of his faculties, physical and mental. He sees the interaction of all that might be if He gave to humans either more or less of the qualities and faculties He has bestowed.

He balances all that might be if He did this or if He did that—and then in His wisdom He decides that this is what man's freedom should be, this is the potential of his intellect, these are to be the qualities of matter, the capabilities of animals, of fish, of birds, of insects, not only of animals as a species but of each individual animal according to the complex interplay of situations and events that He foresees will take place.

This is the meaning of the old saying that "this is the best of all possible worlds." It is the world that God has foreseen, permitted, and provided for. If man perfectly followed God's will, the world would be quite a different place. But God will not force man to follow His will. He will not coerce man to goodness—He even left him free to crucify Jesus.

But God sees the effect of every sin just as He sees the effect of every act of virtue. And he provides for it. He permits sin, but He does not permit sin to wipe out His plan. Sin will never conquer. He is in charge. He permits the evil of sin and only for a greater good. The greater good in the cruel passion and death of Jesus is the love with which Jesus accepts His humanity and the trials and pains it brings upon Him. Out of man's greatest sin flows redemption, the Mystical Body of Christ, the Church. Out of this most horrible of deeds flows the great love-act of Jesus, God and man, toward His Father.

God sees man's freedom as so good that He will not recall or take it away even when man uses it to crucify His own Son—but out of that crucifixion He draws an incomparable good.

It is heartening to see God's providence in this way. We see Him permitting the effects and the consequences of sin to come down hard on mankind—but we know He will draw good out of it. He has provided—it is not left to chance. We may suffer for our neglects and omissions and our malice and hatred, and this is just and right, and it is in accordance with God's providing. But in the end sin will not conquer. Man can rise out of sin to immense heights of goodness.

If man does not so rise, it is his own doing. Man condemns himself. Man says: "I will not serve." It is man's choice, a free choice. God does not will that man should choose evil—but He foresees it, He permits it (for a greater good) and He provides for it (that good can flow out of it). So today when we are looking out on a world in which hunger and violence and cruel war and selfishness abound—when we are not at all certain but that nuclear war may wipe out much of civilization, we have this consolation—that God has foreseen it, that He permits it, and that He has provided for it so that it will contribute ultimately to the victory of goodness over evil, of God over Satan. The end of it all will be great and good, perhaps not in our time or that of our children—but eventually, sometime, because God has provided and God will not be mocked, and God *is* in charge.

Chapter Sixteen

He Must Become More And More

In the preceding chapters we have tried to show that:

All are called to holiness.

Holiness consists in being some*one* rather than in doing some*thing*.

The someone each of us is called to be is unique. This means that we must strive to be not saints in general, but rather the particular saints God intends.

Holiness consists, therefore, in being completely what we are in the best possible way.

To be completely what we are we must let God lead us, moment by moment and step by step, uniting our will with His in every present moment of our existence.

If once again the question is, "how?" the answer is— spiritual recollection.

And it is precisely here that many of us, well-intentioned and apostolic-minded as we may be, encounter one of our most formidable hurdles.

We have no time. We have no time set aside, that is, in which to regularly practice recollection. The monk in the monastery, the nun in the convent, have their hours for Holy Mass, for the Divine Office, for meditation, and for other spiritual exercises. The secular priest has his daily Mass schedule, the Liturgy of the Hours, and incentives for meditation. As many a married person has noted, more or less enviously, priests can even fall back on the office to escape gracefully from tiresome social functions.

The laity are pretty much on their own. Daily Mass for the priest, while not a strict obligation, is certainly "part of the job." For the laity, it's an extra, over and above the job. Neither are they obligated to pray the Office, to do spiritual reading or to meditate; on the contrary, it is a bit difficult to fit spiritual exercises with any regularity into workaday schedules.

We have no place. There are no chapels in our homes, no churches next door. We can't, generally speaking, "duck in" at any break in the day to pray the rosary, make the Way of the Cross, or spend five minutes before the Blessed Sacrament.

We have few reminders. In the factories, offices, and stores where so many of us work, crucifixes, statues, and religious paintings do not abound. In the home or outside of it, no tinkling bell summons us to worship. Even the church bells that used to call out "time for the Angelus" are stilled in many of our cities.

Yet there is another side, and we would be unfair not to recognize it. True, we have no designated hours for prayer, but we in the United States undoubtedly have more free time, in general, than any generation that has ever lived, anywhere. We have longer weekends and shorter workdays, bigger vacations and earlier retirement—adding up to more leisure than some of us know what to do with.

While we have less access to places of worship than the clergy and others in the religious life, churches and chapels are more favorably located in terms of time and convenience than ever before. And the noon, afternoon, and evening Masses, together with the relaxed regulations for the Communion fast, bring the Mass and the sacraments within comparatively easy range.

As for reminders, while the bells in our town may no longer ring out for Angelus, we are far more fortunate than earlier generations in the religious books, magazines, newspapers, and pamphlets everywhere available, to say nothing of the radio and television programs of religious significance that can be ours for the turning of a knob.

Admitting all this, the time-place-reminder situation still constitutes a mammoth handicap to the soul in search of recollection. The difficulty is that though leisure, in the sense of time away from the job, has grown, the attractive secular demands upon that leisure have more than kept pace. Though our access to churches, to the Mass and the sacraments is favorable, our fevered pace all too often causes us to rush into a noontime Mass at the Gospel and leave it immediately after

Communion, wondering if we've done right to steal these precious moments from our crowded lunch period.

And though we have the vast advantage of a well-advanced Catholic literature and press, we have also to contend with the almost overwhelming pressure of a materialistic secular press, the flamboyant sensualism of the paperbacks, the movies that become more pornographic every year, and the trash that saturates most of a normal evening's watching on television.

We live surrounded by noise, but recollection thrives only in quiet. Our world is in turmoil, but recollection demands serenity. Violence assails us as the crime statistics demonstrate, but recollection cries for peace. The atomic age threatens mankind with an unbelievable horror, and this the spirit of recollection can only abhor.

Enmeshed as we are in this net of fevered living, buffeted by noise and turmoil, bereft of peace and quiet, spinning frantically in a whirlpool of anxieties, how can we live a recollected life?

The spirit of recollection requires that we live with God in the back of our minds, so to speak, all day long. But isn't this asking too much? How can a mother be recollected when simultaneously the baby is crying, the telephone is ringing, somebody is at the front door, and the smell of the oven indicates that the casserole must come out—this minute!

How can a person be recollected driving a car through traffic, with income-tax problems, payroll schedules, and a painful phone call that must be made within the next thirty minutes, preying on his mind?

Or to veer away from extremes, how can recollection be practiced in a world in which exterior cares absorb so much attention, and even our leisure more and more consists of a hectic round of meetings, socializing, and that host of activities that fall under the category of "getting ahead"?

The answer is that recollection can be practiced and achieved even in such a world; indeed, it must be if we are to live as God would have us live.

We who have no time, must make time for the health of our souls. Time for daily Mass, to the extent that it does not interfere with our duties. Time for spiritual reading, again fitted into the demands of vocation and circumstances. But above all, time for what Teresa of Avila called the prayer of recollection.

Like a businessman lopping off departments of his enterprise that give no indication of ever being able to pull their own weight, we have to cut out of our lives those occupations and activities unnecessary to our state of life, that overburden us, agitate us, and in the words of Father Joseph Schryvers, C.SS.R., "dry up the heart, and finally bring disgust for the interior life."

We must exercise will power, and take inventory of the hours of our day. What portion of our time is given to activities corresponding closely to the duties of our vocation? What portion is given to activities that correspond loosely or are of indifferent value to our vocation? And what portion is given over to things totally extraneous? Specifically, do we devote far too many precious hours to television entertainment, light reading, idle conversation, social pleasures, or other forms of relaxation?

Chapter Seventeen

"We Need No Wings"

To lead a well-ordered spiritual life, we must weed out enough unessentials to provide time for what Father Schryvers calls "that peaceful self-possession which is the basis of the perfect life." And the core of this self-possession is to be found in the prayer of recollection.

This is simply a withdrawal of our attention from exterior things in order to give our attention to God. "It is called recollection," Teresa of Avila says, "because the soul collects together all the faculties and enters within itself to be with its God." In this prayer, she explains, "it is well to reflect for a time . . . (but) we must sometimes remain by His side with our minds hushed in silence. If we can, we should occupy ourselves in looking upon Him Who is looking at us; keep Him company; talk with Him; pray to Him; humble ourselves before Him; have our delight in Him."

And further: "Speak with Him as with a Father, a Brother, a Lord, and a Spouse—and sometimes in one way and sometimes in another, He will teach you what you must do to please Him."

Having made time, what shall we do to find a place? Must we go to a church or chapel in which to practice this prayer of recollection? Again, let us listen to the saint of Avila:

> Remember how St. Augustine tells us about his seeking God in many places and eventually finding Him within himself? Do you suppose it is of little importance that a soul which is so often distracted should come to understand this truth and to find that, in order to speak to its Eternal Father or to take its delight in Him, it has no need to go to Heaven or to speak in a loud voice? However quietly we speak, He is so near that He will hear us; we need no wings to go in search of Him but have only to find a place where we can be alone and look upon Him present within us.

Nor is it even absolutely necessary that we be physically alone. Interior solitude can be had anywhere, so long as we make an effort to withdraw our minds even if only for the moment from what is going on around us and focus our attention on the indwelling God.

Out of these periods of prayer will develop the habit of turning to God at intervals during the day, and these turnings will grow in number until eventually we may come to a recollection that "sees" God in all that occurs, task by task, event by event, almost moment by moment. Thus the prayer of recollection will be increasingly renewed by continual glances of the mind Godward until it becomes the thread that ties together all the happenings of all our days.

This may come to pass slowly or rapidly, depending partly on our faithfulness but ultimately, of course, on God's favor. As Teresa expresses it, however, "If you become accustomed to having Him at your side, and if He sees that you love Him to be there and are always trying to please Him, you will never be able, as we put it, to send Him away."

Recollection, all the spiritual writers agree, must be wooed; it cannot be forced. It would be sheer foolishness to say to ourselves: All this day I am going to force myself to be aware of the presence of God within me. That way lies only disappointment, irritability, and eventually even disgust with the whole idea. This does not mean that a resolution is fruitless, nor that we should not deliberately turn our attention to God. Such turnings, however, should never be agitated, strained, or forced, but rather calm though firm, tranquil though definite, leisurely, unhurried, gentle.

Ejaculatory prayer has been recommended at least from the time of Augustine as a most important aid to recollection. In fact Francis de Sales wrote: "As the great work of devotion consists in the exercise of spiritual recollection and ejaculatory prayers, the want of all other prayers may be supplied by them; but the loss of these can scarcely be repaired by any other means. Without them we cannot properly lead the contemplative life, and we can but poorly lead active life. Without them repose would be but idleness and labor vexation."

Being spiritually recollected does not mean, of course, that we are consciously and directly thinking of God all day long. It does mean that we think of Him in this way often, perhaps only in quickly raising our heart or glancing, as it were, in His direction. But it means further that we are never very far removed from a consciousness of Him in the back of our minds. We are aware of Him somewhat as a lover is aware of being in the same room or same house as his beloved even when he is not directly thinking of her, much less speaking to or looking at her.

And just as the lover never has to make a resolution that he will think of his beloved, so with the recollected soul. The fact that we desire to be aware of God—that we are attracted to thinking of Him—that we want it with a kind of quiet longing, this is the secret of recollection.

Having achieved at least the beginnings of recollection, we find it no longer so necessary to fight off the distracting details of our daily living. Instead of excluding them, it becomes possible to make use of them. Take our work, for example. How often have we set out to "sanctify" our work by offering it to God, by submitting to its monotony and drudgery for His sake? This is good and undoubtedly profitable. But recollection leads us to permit our work to sanctify us. We see it as coming from the hand of the Lord, hearing in it His voice, accepting it as His gift, knowing that it comes to us with His love.

Chapter Eighteen

"If Only . . ."

In a thousand different ways God uses suffering to shape, strengthen, and purify our souls. "Some persons," writes Father Joseph Schryvers, "understood this loving conduct of God and let themselves be formed as He wills. Others are astonished; they murmur, and shrink from the divine operations."

Is this not the point of separation between the heroic and the mediocre Christian? "The trial is the same, the occasion is the same; the only difference is in the interior disposition."

Never is this point of separation more sharply defined than in time of sickness. Making all due allowance for the fact that the threshold of pain and the tendency to worry differ widely from person to person, the response to illness, especially serious illness, is often the acid test of one's submission to the will of God. How difficult it is to accept the particular sickness that befalls us without seeking to cut the pattern to suit ourselves. How often we say, "I wouldn't mind being sick if only it didn't interfere with my work." Or—"If only it didn't last so long."

Or—"I wish I weren't so weak." Or—"If only this headache were not a part of it." Or—"If only the meals in this hospital weren't served cold." Or—"If only I could be somewhere else."

These, actually, are not serious complaints. Often they are little more than conversational gambits. But sometimes, especially when the siege stretches into months, complaints become rebellion. This is tragic. But the tragedy is not in the discomfort rebellion produces in the patient and everyone around him; it is rather in the waste of God's best gift.

How differently the heroes of holiness have acted. First, they've not feared the onslaught of sickness. If sickness happens to be part of God's plan, so be it. Reasonable care of one's health, yes; but beyond this, "behold the servant, or handmaid, of the Lord."

Heroic souls have allowed God to engrave on their hearts the beautiful words of the marriage ceremony that applies to all sacrifice—"Love can make it easy, and perfect love can make it a joy."

Therefore, when illness besets them, when their bodies cry for rest and their work seems more than they can manage; when they are tormented by worry that seems beyond their power to control; when they are subjected to ridicule and have lost the respect of others; when grief assaults them and threatens to overcome them, and they momentarily feel that even God Himself has deserted them and their broken, abandoned souls are totally unable to bear another wound, then perhaps God recalls to their minds these sentiments of St. Francis de Sales:

God in His divine wisdom
has from all eternity beheld the cross
He bestows upon you—
His precious gift
from His heart.

He contemplated this cross
with His all-knowing eye
before bestowing it upon you.

He pondered over it
with His divine mind;

He examined it
with His all-wise justice;
with His loving mercy
He warmed it through and through.

And with both His hands
He weighed it
to determine if it be
one ounce too heavy for you.

He blessed it with His all-holy Name
With His grace He anointed it.
And with His consolation He perfumed it.

And then once more
He considered you
and your courage.

Finally, it comes from heaven
as a special message of God
to you;
an alms
of the all-merciful love of God
for you.

With such a sublime concept of the divine love is it any wonder that St. Francis could say in another place: "If jealousy could enter into the realm of eternal love, the angels themselves would envy the sufferings of God for man, and those of man for God?"

For the heroic soul, then, the cross is not something to be avoided. Neither, generally speaking, is it something to be sought. Rather, the cross is to be accepted, and borne exactly as God presents it at every present moment.

Particularly is this true of our major, or predominant, cross. As we go through life, the trials and sufferings are many and varied. Usually, at any given time, some one cross, trial, problem, or difficulty predominates. This year it may be poverty, next year ill health, either afflicting us or one dear to us. For youngsters it may be the inability to get into college, failure to make the team, lack of popularity in the group. For any of us, it may be a physical handicap: a speech difficulty that causes acute embarrassment and hinders professional progress; defective hearing; sudden loss of a limb; partial or total blindness.

Whatever the cross and however burdensome it may be, it is intended to be a seedbed of virtue; and it *can* be. Since it is our major cross, it is the major mortification God has selected or has permitted us to have as of this moment. It is the key to holiness that He Himself holds out to us. In patiently, willingly, lovingly bearing it, we are in effect carrying a sliver, or more, of Christ's own Cross. We are sharing in His atonement, making up, as St. Paul put it, "what is lacking in the sufferings of Christ."

Our major cross will increase our faith—if we believe that it comes from God.

It will increase our trust—if we can realize that God knows best.

Our love—if we bear it with love.

Humility—if it makes us see ourselves as we really are.

Prayerfulness—if we ask God's help to cope with it.

Generosity—if we offer it up for others.

Patience—if we accept it serenely.

Fortitude—if we bear it bravely.

Prudence—if it keeps us from attempting more than our handicap permits.

Indeed it is true: in the cross is the seed of every virtue.

Chapter Nineteen

Our Love Is Proved
by Action

To insist that holiness resides in what we are rather than in what we accomplish is not to say that it is a private affair. On the contrary, holiness is so little a private affair that it demands an apostolate. And heroic holiness demands a heroic apostolate.

This can be a frightening thought; but surely it's a realistic one. The essence of holiness is love, therefore it has love's characteristics; and what is more characteristic of love than its dynamism, its aliveness, its need to express itself?

See how the heroic holiness (love) of Paul and Francis Xavier drove them to magnificent missionary endeavor; and how the holiness of Thomas Aquinas found expression in the divine *Summa*.

It was the heroic love (holiness) of Francis of Assisi that brought forth the great Franciscan orders, and the love of

Vincent de Paul and Peter Claver that "made them" minister
to the poor, the sick, the enslaved.

Heroic love—loving holiness—is channeled into different activities in different saints: in Mother Cabrini it led to
schools, orphanages, hospitals; in John Bosco to instructing
the young; in Charles Borromeo to founding the Confrater-
nity of Christian Doctrine; in Catherine Labouré to introduc-
ing the Miraculous Medal.

Heroic apostolates, all. And consequently discouraging
to you and me? Never! For though heroic holiness demands
a heroic apostolate, the caliber of the latter is not necessarily
measured in terms of manifest achievement. How indebted we
are to Thérèsè for conclusively demonstrating this truth!

Here was a young woman who taught by the minutest
details of her life what all the saints have had to learn, namely
that "Our Lord doesn't ask for great achievements, only for
self-surrender and for gratitude . . . it isn't that He wants us to
do this or that, He wants us to love Him."

But like all love, Thérèsè's needed "to be proved by action."
Indeed, so insatiable was her love that "to be betrothed" to
our Lord as a Carmelite, to become through union with Him
"a mother of souls," even this was too little for her vaulting
ambition. She wrote in words addressed to our Lord Himself,
"I feel as if I were called to be a fighter, a priest, an apostle,
a doctor, a martyr; as if I could never satisfy the needs of my
nature without performing, for Your sake, every kind of heroic
action at once."

"I'd like to travel all over the world," she continued, "making Your name known and planting Your cross on heathen

soil; only I shouldn't be content with one particular mission. I should want to be preaching the gospel on all five continents and in the most distant lands, all at once. And even then it wouldn't do, carrying on my mission for a limited number of years; I should want to have been a missionary ever since the creation, and go on being a missionary till the world came to an end."

So it was that her heroic love gave to the Little Flower a heroic apostolate; that without leaving the cloister she became, after her death, the heavenly patroness, with Francis Xavier, of the Catholic missions.

Francis Xavier made history. The Little Flower, so far as the world knew, created hardly a ripple. Yet because of the common denominator of love, they share the exalted privilege of being patron and patroness of the mission apostolate. How encouraging this is!

Even if holiness were not apostolic by nature, our Lord would have made it so by His last words before he ascended to His Father. "You shall be my witnesses in Jerusalem and in all Judea and Samaria and even to the very ends of the earth."

Though He spoke to the apostles, popes, and bishops, from Peter to His Holiness John XXIII, we have never ceased interpreting this command as one involving an apostolate of the whole Church. Every Catholic, then, from the beginnings of the Church until now, has had a duty, conferred by Baptism and Confirmation, to be an apostle.

It is in our own century, however, that the layman's call to be an apostle has become particularly insistent. Pius X: "What is the one thing that the Church today needs and will need in modern times more than anything else? An intelligent, informed, holy, and active laity." And again, "Give me in every parish a handful of laymen—alert, well informed, devoted—and I will change the face of the earth."

Pope Pius XI: "It is necessary that all men be apostles—None can remain inactive."

Pope Pius XII: "The consecration of the world is essentially the work of the laymen themselves."

Pope John XXIII: "Take action, then, boldly and with confidence. Heavenly light will shine upon you. God's help will be granted you."

Why? Why does our age demand more apostolic effort of you and me than other eras demanded of their laity?

Surely it is caused in part by a widespread decay of morals. In many quarters today there is little more sense of sin or of shame than existed in that period of moral nadir just before the Incarnation.

Even more surely it is caused by a decay of faith. Now has come to pass Cardinal Newman's prophecy of a century ago.

"All times," he wrote, "have their special trials which others have not. I think that the trials which lie before us are such as would appall and make dizzy even such courageous hearts as Athanasius, Gregory I, or Gregory VII . . .

"The special peril of the time before us is the spread of that plague of infidelity, that the Apostles and Our Lord Himself have predicted as the worst calamity of the last times of the Church."

Not only is faith in Christ's divinity being eroded, but even belief in God's existence at all.

Do not say this has always been the case. It has indeed been true of individuals—but today we live in a world largely, perhaps predominantly, irreligious and proud of it; and Christianity has never faced that situation before. In other days there was superstition, but not infidelity; not a complete casting off of the idea of religion, of unseen powers that govern the world. Even among the skeptics of Athens, Paul acknowledged the appeal of an unknown god.

And partly the demands upon us of the laity stem from progress in literacy and communication. In earlier generations, to believers and unbelievers alike, even to those who hated the Church he represented, the priest stood intellectually tall.

Now the unbeliever no longer looks to the priest. More and more, only the lay believer can catch his eye and command his ear. And this is why the consecration of the world is essentially the work of the laity, "of men who are intimately a part of the economic and social life, and who participate in the government and legislative assemblies" (Pius XII).

Chapter Twenty

"A Chosen Race"

What must we do? How is the holiness of the lay person to be expressed in an apostolate?

It seems strange in a way, but the fact is that the basic set of instructions for the lay apostle—still applicable today—were set down by Peter in his first epistle. He tells us what we are: "A chosen race, a royal priesthood, a holy nation, a people that is God's possession, that you may proclaim the excellence of Him Who called you out of darkness."

There must be about us an aura of calm serenity, fitting one who has abandoned his will to that of the all-loving, all-wise, all-powerful God. In an age of unrest, doubt, and fear, we must be rocks of confidence.

Our faces must exhibit the gentle strength that is the hallmark of holiness. There must be in our manner such an undercurrent of joy and gladness that others will be happy to be near us.

He tells us how to act: "See that your conduct among the pagans is praiseworthy, so that . . . they may . . . glorify God when He grants them the grace of conversion."

On the street, in the home, at the office, on the playground, at the beach, on the golf course and tennis courts, in the hospital, the university, the nursery school, in the courts and the prisons, in the theaters and libraries, we must carry Christ to the world. We must introduce Him by our example, recommend Him by our life, extend His kingdom by our prayers.

He tells us how to speak: "Be always ready to give an answer to everyone who asks you the basis of the hope you cherish. Do this, however, with meekness and reserve."

The atmosphere of charity must be our mantle. Our actions and attitudes must point quietly to one fact: that we love our neighbor as Christ loves us. How frequently it happens that our manner offends. How easy it is to become angry, impatient, and resentful, when others do not agree with us.

We must be ready to "give an answer." It is no excuse to say we are not prepared. True, the Catholic who goes into the world expecting to hold his own in religious discussions by parroting the pat answers of the catechism is due for a rude, disappointing, and painful awakening. We have precise positions to uphold and to explain in terms that make sense to intelligent, if doubting, Thomases. It seems to take considerably more than a diploma or a degree from the typical Catholic high school or college to fit us for the task. If this is true, the fault lies partly at the door of educators, but partly also at the door of parents. Some educators act as if all the rights of educating were theirs. Many parents act as if none of the responsibility of educating were theirs. No wonder neither educators nor parents are satisfied with the product.

If we ourselves are ill-prepared, we have a certain duty to train ourselves in how to take advantage of opportunities to speak up for the hope we cherish, in how to approach others, in letter writing, in how to do all that an apostle should do—gracefully.

Peter tells us to share our talents: "Each of you should use what endowments he has received in the service of others; as good stewards of the manifold bounty of God."

It used to be customary to tithe out of one's income. But it has always been more important and is so today to tithe out of our time. Nobody can tell anyone else how much of his time or of his income he should devote to apostolic endeavors. But it is certain that we are obligated to be reasonably generous with both.

Each of us is free to choose apostolic endeavors that fit his ability and circumstances—CCD, family life, interracial justice, Legion of Mary, Holy Name, Sodality—but we *must* choose. If circumstances prevent our devoting ourselves to outside activities, we can at least devote some time to study, spiritual reading, writing letters, or to the best and most effective apostolate of all—the apostolate of prayer.

"Beloved," Peter says, "rejoice to the extent that you share in the sufferings of Christ."

To be an apostle will not be accomplished without difficulty. Our Lord did not promise to spare us work and trials. He promised only to make our burden light. We will meet with rebuffs even as He did. We may have to endure calumny, false charges, scandal as He endured the charge that He was a devil. Some of our friends may turn against us and wound us as He was wounded when His friends deserted Him.

Yet all the while He will be with us. Deep within our souls we will know that our sufferings are not worthy to be compared with the joy of being His apostle.

"Above all things," Peter writes, "practice constant love among yourselves; it wins forgiveness for many sins." In this, perhaps the best known of Peter's admonitions, is the supreme test of today's apostle.

How speedily we are entrapped by pride and self-preferment when we are opposed even by those of our own faith, those who do not choose to march side by side with us in our particular apostolate. Surely this is an indication that our apostolate is more of ourselves than of our Lord. Christ told us to expect opposition. Why become angry when it comes? It is all too easy to forget that God asks us not to succeed in our apostolate but only to try so that He can take from our efforts what He wants and fill up in them what is lacking for their success.

The cooperation of the laity with the hierarchy, according to Pope Pius XII, "has never been so necessary" as today. "It seems to us," he said, "that Christ is repeating to each of you, the question He put to Peter: 'Do you love me?' and He is looking each of you straight in the eye, hoping to read there the sincerity of your reply: 'Yes, Lord, You know I love You.'"

And to Christian women he addressed these words particularly appropriate to these chapters: "Never in the course of humanity have events required on the part of woman so much initiative and daring, so much fidelity, moral strength, spirit of sacrifice and endurance of all kinds of suffering—in a word, so much heroism."

Holiness *demands* expression—an apostolate. Have you found yours? Are you working at it?

Chapter Twenty-One

We Must Do It

The thoughts we have been presenting are not novel. They have all been designed to indicate that what Francis de Sales said three-and-a-half centuries ago remains true today: that "a strong, resolute soul can live in the midst of the world without embracing worldly ideas, that sources of holiness can be found in the hardships of the world, and that one can live among the flames of earthly desires without burning one's wings." Indeed, it is by bearing witness to Christ in precisely this world and in our particular occupation and circumstances—by being, in short, completely what we are—that holiness, even heroic holiness, can and must be achieved.

We must want precisely what God wants for us—no more, no less—here and hereafter. Thérèse demonstrated this by writing in her famed *Act of Oblation*, "I desire to fulfill perfectly Thy will, and to reach the degree of glory Thou hast prepared for me in Thy kingdom." The heroic soul therefore desires exactly that role in the world, in the Church, and even in heaven, that God has destined for it—no more, no less.

But surely over the centuries some formula, some secret, some method must have been developed for achieving sanctity. The only formula, the only secret the saints have been able to prescribe is to love God. This is both the means to sanctity and its end; the means because it is the only way to go to God, the end because sanctity is nothing other than a heroic love of God. Because each moment and each act of loving God makes us love Him more, the means inevitably leads to the end. "If you really want to love God," Francis said, "go on and love Him more and more. Never look back. Move forward constantly. Begin as a humble apprentice and the very power of love will draw you on to become a master in the art."

The "method" the spiritual doctors offer, then, might be summed up in two words: Do it! Instead of trying to find out how we can learn to love God, it is far better to begin to practice loving Him, far better to do it.

Although there is no precise formula for attaining sanctity—because sanctification depends on God's action—there are certain essentials of attitude on our part that will render us receptive to the divine action. These essentials can be signified by the two words just referred to: Do it! Four letters: D-O-I-T, each letter standing for one of the essentials.

The first step toward loving God is to desire to love Him.

No one will ever be a saint who does not want to be holy—who does not want it with a deep and abiding desire. God implants this desire but we ourselves are charged with keeping it alive. The saints *desired* holiness, some of them from early childhood. Teresa was a little girl of seven when she set off with her brother, Rodrigo, hoping to reach the country of the Moors, there to be martyred. An uncle overtook the children and brought them home. But the little Teresa offered the totally logical explanation that she had run away, "I want to see God, and to see Him we must die."

Having failed in this first endeavor, the little Teresa turned to other ways. She built "little hermitages" in an orchard at home. Later she decided to become a nun, but her father refused permission. After a period that probably lasted many months, she left home early one morning with one of her brothers, he to enter the Dominicans, she to become a Carmelite. When her father saw the extent of her desire, he made no further objection but yielded his full consent. Teresa, at the time, was twenty years old.

Her desire to "see God" is reminiscent of the question another future saint kept putting to the monks of Monte Cassino. Young Thomas of Aquino asked over and over, "What is God?", foreshadowing his desire to know and love Him.

The Little Flower, Thérèsè, was equally intent on seeking God. Like Teresa, she had to overcome formidable obstacles, not from her father but from Church authorities because of her tender age. Nevertheless, she entered the Carmel of Lisieux at the age of fifteen. She states matter-of-factly in that section of her autobiography addressed to Mother Marie de Gonzague, "As you know, dear Mother, I've always wished that I could be a saint."

And at least one of the saints, whose name I fail to recall, is said to have departed his home leaving behind a note: "Gone away to be a saint."

Desire is different by far from a whim. Some persons say, "I'd give my right arm to play the piano." Actually, they wouldn't give even fifteen minutes a day to learn to play the piano. True desire is that quality that the football coach often sees exemplified in undersized kids: a burning drive to make the team, a passion, a consuming want, a hunger that refuses to take no for an answer. That it has its counterpart in the spiritual life is evident in the writings and actions of a multitude of saints; for example, in the constant day and night longing of Catherine of Siena for Holy Communion.

Desire remains the starting point of sanctity, no matter how old we become. It grows as holiness grows. Thus, Teresa could write at the age of sixty-two, "I am very old and tired now, though I still have good desires."

The second essential is a kind of optimism that is apparently a universal quality of the saints. It was not for nothing that Teresa could not abide a "sad saint."

The optimism of the saints is compounded of two basic sentiments: of myself I can do nothing; with God there is nothing I can not do. Thérèse, on comparing herself to the saints and concluding that they were like "great mountains" while she was only "an insignificant grain of sand," nevertheless, was not discouraged. As she herself relates, "I said to myself: 'God wouldn't inspire us with ambitions that can't be realized. Obviously there's nothing great to be made of me, so it must be possible for me to aspire to sanctity in spite of my insignificance. I've got to take myself just as I am, with all my imperfections; but somehow I shall have to find out a little way, all of my own, which will be a direct short-cut to heaven.'"

What superb optimism, trust, confidence, call it what you will.

Yet such optimism is not misplaced, since it is placed in the omnipotent. Did not Paul write to the Philippians that God, who had begun His good work in them, would continue to perfect it? And did not Francis de Sales explain that such should be our confidence in God as to believe that He would "rather work a miracle than fail in giving her [the humble soul] the power to accomplish what she attempts, because she undertakes it not relying on her own strength but on the gifts which God has bestowed on her"?

Our confidence must be grounded on the infinite goodness of God, knowing that if we place all in His hands He will provide. After all, we are God's sons and daughters. We sometimes reflect on the wonder of having God for our Father, but seldom on what it means to be His son, of what we should be doing and feeling because we are sons and daughters. The heroically holy soul has the confidence a child of God should have.

What have we to fear from the elements? We are His sons.

What have we to fear from earthly creatures? We are His sons.

What shall we fear from other men? We are His sons.

What have we to fear from Satan himself? We are God's sons.

As sons and daughters, princes and princesses of an omnipotent king, our trust should be unbounded, our love unlimited.

Desire, or the will to be a saint, and optimism, or the trust that God will provide, are only the groundwork. We must build on them by initiating action, by taking positive steps in the direction of sanctity and holiness. In this respect, spiritual goals are no different than other objectives. How many times have we desired to do something—and believed we could—but for one reason or another never took the first step and as a result found our desire cooling, then dying?

Never does God call anyone without providing the capacity to respond. If ever we have felt impelled to surrender ourselves completely to Him—and who has not?—then we may be sure that He has invited us to sainthood.

Where we fail is in holding back our assent. Just as the alcoholic takes the first essential step toward conquering his affliction by admitting with conviction: I *am* an alcoholic; so our first great stride toward holiness is made when we say with earnest honesty, "Yes, my God, I *want* to be a saint."

It is this that so many of us put off so long. We brush aside God's call, perhaps deliberately, burying ourselves in business or pleasure or worldly pursuits. We turn away, saying in effect, "I'll think about being a saint tomorrow."

The third essential, therefore, is *initiative,* making a definite start. Francis de Sales places great store on a decision to give one's whole being over to God. In his *Introduction to the Devout Life,* he provides a formal act of consecration for the soul intent on living the devout life. He regards it as a most solemn occasion, one to be preceded by much deep and prayerful consideration and accompanied by a reception of the sacraments. The heart of his act of consecration consists of the following total dedication: "Turning myself toward my most gracious and merciful God, I desire, purpose, determine, and am irrevocably resolved to serve and love Him now and forever. To this end, I give and consecrate to Him my spirit with all its faculties, my soul with all its powers, my heart with all its affections, and my body with all its senses, protesting that I will nevermore abuse any part of my being against His divine will and sovereign majesty, to whom I offer up and sacrifice myself in spirit, to be forever His loyal, obedient, and faithful creature, without ever revoking or repenting this my act and deed."

A similar total dedication is Thérèse's oblation in which she offered herself as a victim of the merciful love of God. This prayer, which was not found until after her death, reposed in a copy of the Gospels she carried with her at all times.

Some such consecration or decision to belong entirely to God is, if not absolutely necessary, at least immensely helpful. Francis made a special point of urging the renewal of the act of consecration each year on its anniversary day, considering it, in a sense, as only less vital to perfection than the day of one's Baptism.

The all-important thing is to begin, to start, to initiate; to set aside time for prayer, and to begin praying; for spiritual reading, and to start reading; for frequent, if not daily, Mass and the sacraments, and to commence them; for one's chosen apostolate, and to initiate it.

And this brings us to the final essential and the final letter in our acrostic: T, for tenacity. Hundreds of millions may combine desire with optimism. Millions may be moved by desire and optimism to initiate. But how many have the tenacity, the fortitude, the perseverance, to carry through to heroic holiness? We must strive for a toughness of spirit that will stick it out against the devil's most dangerous tool, discouragement.

The essence of this tenacity appears to be the preservation of a great and holy calmness of mind that, in turn, rests upon complete self-abandonment to whatever God wills for us. Though our lives may be a continual warfare, our role is to preserve a peaceful spirit, to guard ourselves against spiritual unrest, and if our heart goes astray, sweetly and gently to call it back to God's presence and His love.

This is all God asks: that we keep turning our souls toward Him, that we give Him our heart's love. This done, the rest is His affair and He carries it to a holy conclusion through the workings within us of the Holy Spirit.

What a consolation it is to realize that to be heroically holy we need only give ourselves into His hands and permit Him to make us completely what we are, completely what He intended us to be. "If we are clever, then to be clever; if we are not clever, then not to be clever; if we are successful, then to be successful; if not successful, then not to succeed; if in good health, then to be healthy; if sickly, then to be sickly; and so on. Perfect simplicity with regard to ourselves; perfect contentment with everything that comes our way; perfect peace of mind in utter self-forgetfulness," says Archbishop Alban Goodier, S.J.

God made us to be great. He made us to be heroic. He made us to be holy. All we need do is welcome the desire to love Him that He gives us; cherish the optimism with which He encourages us; initiate the action to which He inspires us; and cling tenaciously to the hope of heroic holiness He holds before us.

We can do it. God Himself is our assurance.

CLARENCE JOSEPH ENZLER (1910–1976), an accomplished speech-writer and speaker, worked for the US Department of Agriculture (USDA) from 1937 to 1972, leaving the department briefly from 1943 to 1945 to serve as the feature editor with the National Catholic Welfare Conference News Service (now known as Catholic News Service). He prepared speeches for eight Secretaries of Agriculture.

A prolific author, he had articles published in many national magazines, including *The Ave Maria*, and wrote several books, including *Everyone's Way of the Cross*, *In the Presence of God*, and *My Other Self*. He held a doctorate from the Catholic University of America. He was a deacon in the Archdiocese of Washington, and his son, Rev. Msgr. John J. Enzler, is president and CEO of Catholic Charities in the same archdiocese.